T0231969

Machine Learning
Pocket Reference
Working with Structured Data
in Python

Matt Harrison

Beijing · Boston · Farnham · Sebastopol · Tokyo

Machine Learning Pocket Reference

by Matt Harrison

Copyright © 2019 Matt Harrison. All rights reserved.

Published by O'Reilly Media, Inc., 1005 Gravenstein Highway North, Sebastopol, CA 95472.

O'Reilly books may be purchased for educational, business, or sales promotional use. Online editions are also available for most titles (*http://oreilly.com*). For more information, contact our corporate/institutional sales department: 800-998-9938 or *corporate@oreilly.com*.

Acquisitions Editor: Rachel Roumeliotis
Development Editor: Nicole Tache
Production Editor: Christopher Faucher
Copyeditor: Sonia Saruba
Proofreader: Christina Edwards
Indexer: WordCo Indexing Services, Inc.
Interior Designer: David Futato
Cover Designer: Karen Montgomery
Illustrator: Rebecca Demarest

September 2019:   First Edition

Revision History for the First Edition
         2019-08-27:   First Release

See *http://oreilly.com/catalog/errata.csp?isbn=9781492047544* for release details.

978-1-492-04754-4

[LSI]

Table of Contents

Preface

Machine learning and data science are very popular right now and are fast-moving targets. I have worked with Python and data for most of my career and wanted to have a physical book that could provide a reference for the common methods that I have been using in industry and teaching during workshops to solve structured machine learning problems.

This book is what I believe is the best collection of resources and examples for attacking a predictive modeling task if you have structured data. There are many libraries that perform a portion of the tasks required and I have tried to incorporate those that I have found useful as I have applied these techniques in consulting or industry work.

Many may lament the lack of deep learning techniques. Those could be a book by themselves. I also prefer simpler techniques and others in industry seem to agree. Deep learning for unstructured data (video, audio, images), and powerful tools like XGBoost for structured data.

I hope this book serves as a useful reference for you to solve pressing problems.

What to Expect

This book gives in-depth examples of solving common structured data problems. It walks through various libraries and models, their trade-offs, how to tune them, and how to interpret them.

The code snippets are meant to be sized such that you can use and adapt them in your own projects.

Who This Book Is For

If you are just learning machine learning, or have worked with it for years, this book should serve as a valuable reference. It assumes some knowledge of Python, and doesn't delve at all into syntax. Rather it shows how to use various libraries to solve real-world problems.

This will not replace an in-depth course, but should serve as a reference of what an applied machine learning course might cover. (Note: The author uses it as a reference for the data analytics and machine learning courses he teaches.)

Conventions Used in This Book

The following typographical conventions are used in this book:

Italic

> Indicates new terms, URLs, email addresses, filenames, and file extensions.

`Constant width`

> Used for program listings, as well as within paragraphs to refer to program elements such as variable or function names, databases, data types, environment variables, statements, and keywords.

TIP

This element signifies a tip or suggestion.

NOTE

This element signifies a general note.

WARNING

This element indicates a warning or caution.

Using Code Examples

Supplemental material (code examples, exercises, etc.) is available at *https://github.com/mattharrison/ml_pocket_reference*.

This book is here to help you get your job done. In general, if example code is offered with this book, you may use it in your programs and documentation. You do not need to contact us for permission unless you're reproducing a significant portion of the code. For example, writing a program that uses several chunks of code from this book does not require permission. Selling or distributing a CD-ROM of examples from O'Reilly books does require permission. Answering a question by citing this book and quoting example code does not require permission. Incorporating a significant amount of example code from this book into your product's documentation does require permission.

We appreciate, but do not require, attribution. An attribution usually includes the title, author, publisher, and ISBN. For example: "*Machine Learning Pocket Reference* by Matt Harrison (O'Reilly). Copyright 2019 Matt Harrison, 978-1-492-04754-4."

If you feel your use of code examples falls outside fair use or the permission given above, feel free to contact us at *permissions@oreilly.com*.

O'Reilly Online Learning

For almost 40 years, *O'Reilly Media* has provided technology and business training, knowledge, and insight to help companies succeed.

Our unique network of experts and innovators share their knowledge and expertise through books, articles, conferences, and our online learning platform. O'Reilly's online learning platform gives you on-demand access to live training courses, in-depth learning paths, interactive coding environments, and a vast collection of text and video from O'Reilly and 200+ other publishers. For more information, please visit *http://oreilly.com*.

How to Contact Us

Please address comments and questions concerning this book to the publisher:

O'Reilly Media, Inc.
1005 Gravenstein Highway North
Sebastopol, CA 95472
800-998-9938 (in the United States or Canada)
707-829-0515 (international or local)
707-829-0104 (fax)

We have a web page for this book, where we list errata, examples, and any additional information. You can access this page at *http://www.oreilly.com/catalog/9781492047544*.

To comment or ask technical questions about this book, send email to *bookquestions@oreilly.com*.

For more information about our books, courses, conferences, and news, see our website at *http://www.oreilly.com*.

Find us on Facebook: *http://facebook.com/oreilly*

Follow us on Twitter: *http://twitter.com/oreillymedia*

Watch us on YouTube: *http://www.youtube.com/oreillymedia*

Acknowledgments

Much thanks to my wife and family for their support. I'm grateful to the Python community for providing a wonderful language and toolset to work with. Nicole Tache has been lovely to work with and provided excellent feedback. My technical reviewers, Mikio Braun, Natalino Busa, and Justin Francis, kept me honest. Thanks!

CHAPTER 1

Introduction

This is not so much an instructional manual, but rather notes, tables, and examples for machine learning. It was created by the author as an additional resource during training, meant to be distributed as a physical notebook. Participants (who favor the physical characteristics of dead-tree material) could add their own notes and thoughts and have a valuable reference of curated examples.

We will walk through classification with structured data. Other common machine learning applications include predicting a continuous value (regression), creating clusters, or trying to reduce dimensionality, among others. This book does not discuss deep learning techniques. While those techniques work well for unstructured data, most recommend the techniques in this book for structured data.

We assume knowledge and familiarity with Python. Learning how to manipulate data using the pandas library (*https:// pandas.pydata.org*) is useful. We have many examples using pandas, and it is an excellent tool for dealing with structured data. However, some of the indexing operations may be confusing if you are not familiar with numpy. Full coverage of pandas could be a book in itself.

Libraries Used

This book uses many libraries. This can be a good thing and a bad thing. Some of these libraries may be hard to install or conflict with other library versions. Do not feel like you need to install all of these libraries. Use "JIT installation" and only install the libraries that you want to use as you need them.

```
>>> import autosklearn, catboost,
category_encoders, dtreeviz, eli5, fancyimpute,
fastai, featuretools, glmnet_py, graphviz,
hdbscan, imblearn, janitor, lime, matplotlib,
missingno, mlxtend, numpy, pandas, pdpbox, phate,
pydotplus, rfpimp, scikitplot, scipy, seaborn,
shap, sklearn, statsmodels, tpot, treeinterpreter,
umap, xgbfir, xgboost, yellowbrick

>>> for lib in [
...      autosklearn,
...      catboost,
...      category_encoders,
...      dtreeviz,
...      eli5,
...      fancyimpute,
...      fastai,
...      featuretools,
...      glmnet_py,
...      graphviz,
...      hdbscan,
...      imblearn,
...      lime,
...      janitor,
...      matplotlib,
...      missingno,
...      mlxtend,
...      numpy,
...      pandas,
...      pandas_profiling,
...      pdpbox,
...      phate,
```

```
...      pydotplus,
...      rfpimp,
...      scikitplot,
...      scipy,
...      seaborn,
...      shap,
...      sklearn,
...      statsmodels,
...      tpot,
...      treeinterpreter,
...      umap,
...      xgbfir,
...      xgboost,
...      yellowbrick,
... ]:
...      try:
...          print(lib.__name__, lib.__version__)
...      except:
...          print("Missing", lib.__name__)
catboost 0.11.1
category_encoders 2.0.0
Missing dtreeviz
eli5 0.8.2
fancyimpute 0.4.2
fastai 1.0.28
featuretools 0.4.0
Missing glmnet_py
graphviz 0.10.1
hdbscan 0.8.22
imblearn 0.4.3
janitor 0.16.6
Missing lime
matplotlib 2.2.3
missingno 0.4.1
mlxtend 0.14.0
numpy 1.15.2
pandas 0.23.4
Missing pandas_profiling
pdpbox 0.2.0
phate 0.4.2
```

```
Missing pydotplus
rfpimp
scikitplot 0.3.7
scipy 1.1.0
seaborn 0.9.0
shap 0.25.2
sklearn 0.21.1
statsmodels 0.9.0
tpot 0.9.5
treeinterpreter 0.1.0
umap 0.3.8
xgboost 0.81
yellowbrick 0.9
```

NOTE

Most of these libraries are easily installed with `pip` or conda. With `fastai` I need to use `pip install --no-deps fastai`. The `umap` library is installed with `pip install umap-learn`. The `janitor` library is installed with `pip install pyjanitor`. The `autosklearn` library is installed with `pip install auto-sklearn`.

I usually use Jupyter for doing an analysis. You can use other notebook tools as well. Note that some, like Google Colab, have preinstalled many of the libraries (though they may be outdated versions).

There are two main options for installing libraries in Python. One is to use `pip` (an acronym for Pip Installs Python), a tool that comes with Python. The other option is to use Anaconda (*https://anaconda.org*). We will introduce both.

Installation with Pip

Before using pip, we will create a sandbox environment to install our libraries into. This is called a virtual environment named env:

```
$ python -m venv env
```

NOTE

On Macintosh and Linux, use python; on Windows, use python3. If Windows doesn't recognize that from the command prompt, you may need to reinstall or fix your install and make sure you check the "Add Python to my PATH" checkbox.

Then you activate the environment so that when you install libraries, they go in the sandbox environment and not in the global Python installation. As many of these libraries change and are updated, it is best to lock down versions on a per-project basis so you know that your code will run.

Here is how we activate the virtual environment on Linux and Macintosh:

```
$ source env/bin/activate
```

You will notice that the prompt is updated, indicating that we are using the virtual environment:

```
(env) $ which python
env/bin/python
```

On Windows, you will need to activate the environment by running this command:

```
C:> env\Scripts\activate.bat
```

Again, you will notice that the prompt is updated, indicating that we are using the virtual environment:

```
(env) C:> where python
env\Scripts\python.exe
```

On all platforms, you can install packages using pip. To install pandas, type:

```
(env) $ pip install pandas
```

Some of the package names are different than the library names. You can search for packages using:

```
(env) $ pip search libraryname
```

Once you have your packages installed, you can create a file with all of the versions of the packages using pip:

```
(env) $ pip freeze > requirements.txt
```

With this requirements.txt file you can easily install the packages into a new virtual environment:

```
(other_env) $ pip install -r requirements.txt
```

Installation with Conda

The conda tool comes with Anaconda and lets us create environments and install packages.

To create an environment named env, run:

```
$ conda create --name env python=3.6
```

To activate this environment, run:

```
$ conda activate env
```

This will update the prompt on both Unix and Windows systems. Now you can search for packages using:

```
(env) $ conda search libraryname
```

To install a package, like pandas, run:

```
(env) $ conda install pandas
```

To create a file with the package requirements in it, run:

```
(env) $ conda env export > environment.yml
```

To install these requirements in a new environment, run:

```
(other_env) $ conda create -f environment.yml
```

WARNING

Some of the libraries mentioned in this book are not available to install from Anaconda's repository. Don't fret. It turns out you can use `pip` inside of a conda environment (no need to create a new virtual environment), and install these using `pip`.

CHAPTER 2

Overview of the Machine Learning Process

Cross-Industry Standard Process for Data Mining (CRISP-DM) is a process for doing data mining. It has several steps that can be followed for continuous improvement. They are:

- Business understanding
- Data understanding
- Data preparation
- Modeling
- Evaluation
- Deployment

Figure 2-1 shows my workflow for creating a predictive model that expands on the CRISP-DM methodology. The walk-through in the next chapter will cover these basic steps.

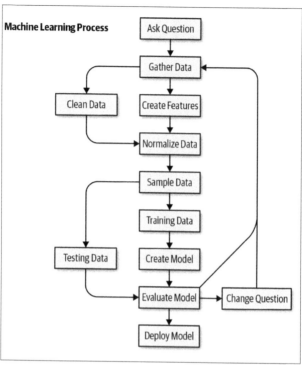

Figure 2-1. Common workflow for machine learning.

CHAPTER 3

Classification Walkthrough: Titanic Dataset

This chapter will walk through a common classification problem using the Titanic dataset (*https://oreil.ly/PjceO*). Later chapters will dive into and expand on the common steps performed during an analysis.

Project Layout Suggestion

An excellent tool for performing exploratory data analysis is Jupyter (*https://jupyter.org*). Jupyter is an open-source notebook environment that supports Python and other languages. It allows you to create *cells* of code or Markdown content.

I tend to use Jupyter in two modes. One is for exploratory data analysis and quickly trying things out. The other is more of a deliverable style where I format a report using Markdown cells and insert code cells to illustrate important points or discoveries. If you aren't careful, your notebooks might need some refactoring and application of software engineering practices (remove globals, use functions and classes, etc.).

The cookiecutter data science package (*https://oreil.ly/86jL3*) suggests a layout to create an analysis that allows for easy reproduction and sharing code.

Imports

This example is based mostly on pandas (*http://pandas.pydata.org/*), scikit-learn (*https://scikit-learn.org/*), and Yellowbrick (*http://www.scikit-yb.org/*). The pandas library gives us tooling for easy data munging. The scikit-learn library has great predictive modeling, and Yellowbrick is a visualization library for evaluating models:

```
>>> import matplotlib.pyplot as plt
>>> import pandas as pd
>>> from sklearn import (
...     ensemble,
...     preprocessing,
...     tree,
... )
>>> from sklearn.metrics import (
...     auc,
...     confusion_matrix,
...     roc_auc_score,
...     roc_curve,
... )
>>> from sklearn.model_selection import (
...     train_test_split,
...     StratifiedKFold,
... )
>>> from yellowbrick.classifier import (
...     ConfusionMatrix,
...     ROCAUC,
... )
>>> from yellowbrick.model_selection import (
...     LearningCurve,
... )
```

Ask a Question

In this example, we want to create a predictive model to answer a question. It will classify whether an individual survives the Titanic ship catastrophe based on individual and trip characteristics. This is a toy example, but it serves as a pedagogical tool for showing many steps of modeling. Our model should be able to take passenger information and predict whether that passenger would survive on the Titanic.

This is a classification question, as we are predicting a label for survival; either they survived or they died.

Terms for Data

We typically train a model with a matrix of data. (I prefer to use pandas DataFrames because it is very nice to have column labels, but numpy arrays work as well.)

For supervised learning, such as regression or classification, our intent is to have a fuction that transforms features into a label. If we were to write this as an algebra formula, it would look like this:

```
y = f(X)
```

X is a matrix. Each row represents a *sample* of data or information about an individual. Every column in X is a *feature*. The output of our function, y, is a vector that contains labels (for classification) or values (for regression) (see Figure 3-1).

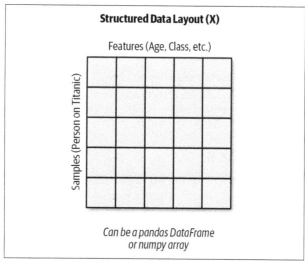

Figure 3-1. Structured data layout.

This is standard naming procedure for naming the data and the output. If you read academic papers or even look at the documentation for libraries, they follow this convention. In Python, we use the variable name X to hold the sample data even though capitalization of variables is a violation of standard naming conventions (PEP 8). Don't worry, everyone does it, and if you were to name your variable x, they might look at you funny. The variable y stores the labels or targets.

Table 3-1 shows a basic dataset with two samples and three features for each sample.

Table 3-1. Samples (rows) and features (columns)

pclass	age	sibsp
1	29	0
1	2	1

Gather Data

We are going to load an Excel file (make sure you have pandas and xlrd[1] installed) with the Titanic features. It has many columns, including a survived column that contains the label of what happened to an individual:

```
>>> url = (
...     "http://biostat.mc.vanderbilt.edu/"
...     "wiki/pub/Main/DataSets/titanic3.xls"
... )
>>> df = pd.read_excel(url)
>>> orig_df = df
```

The following columns are included in the dataset:

- pclass - Passenger class (1 = 1st, 2 = 2nd, 3 = 3rd)
- survival - Survival (0 = No, 1 = Yes)
- name - Name
- sex - Sex
- age - Age
- sibsp - Number of siblings/spouses aboard
- parch - Number of parents/children aboard
- ticket - Ticket number
- fare - Passenger fare
- cabin - Cabin
- embarked - Point of embarkation (C = Cherbourg, Q = Queenstown, S = Southampton)
- boat - Lifeboat
- body - Body identification number

---

1 Even though we don't directly call this library, when we load an Excel file, pandas leverages it behind the scenes.

- home.dest - Home/destination

Pandas can read this spreadsheet and convert it into a Data-Frame for us. We will need to spot-check the data and ensure that it is OK for performing analysis.

Clean Data

Once we have the data, we need to ensure that it is in a format that we can use to create a model. Most scikit-learn models require that our features be numeric (integer or float). In addition, many models fail if they are passed missing values (NaN in pandas or numpy). Some models perform better if the data is *standardized* (given a mean value of 0 and a standard deviation of 1). We will deal with these issues using pandas or scikit-learn. In addition, the Titanic dataset has *leaky* features.

Leaky features are variables that contain information about the future or target. There's nothing bad in having data about the target, and we often have that data during model creation time. However, if those variables are not available when we perform a prediction on a new sample, we should remove them from the model as they are leaking data from the future.

Cleaning the data can take a bit of time. It helps to have access to a subject matter expert (SME) who can provide guidance on dealing with outliers or missing data.

```
>>> df.dtypes
pclass          int64
survived        int64
name            object
sex             object
age             float64
sibsp           int64
parch           int64
ticket          object
fare            float64
cabin           object
embarked        object
```

```
boat            object
body            float64
home.dest       object
dtype: object
```

We typically see `int64`, `float64`, `datetime64[ns]`, or `object`. These are the types that pandas uses to store a column of data. `int64` and `float64` are numeric types. `datetime64[ns]` holds date and time data. `object` typically means that it is holding string data, though it could be a combination of string and other types.

When reading from CSV files, pandas will try to coerce data into the appropriate type, but will fall back to `object`. Reading data from spreadsheets, databases, or other systems may provide better types in the DataFrame. In any case, it is worthwhile to look through the data and ensure that the types make sense.

Integer types are typically fine. Float types might have some missing values. Date and string types will need to be converted or used to feature engineer numeric types. String types that have low cardinality are called categorical columns, and it might be worthwhile to create dummy columns from them (the `pd.get_dummies` function takes care of this).

NOTE

Up to pandas 0.23, if the type is `int64`, we are guaranteed that there are no missing values. If the type is `float64`, the values might be all floats, but also could be integer-like numbers with missing values. The pandas library converts integer values that have missing numbers to floats, as this type supports missing values. The `object` typically means string types (or both string and numeric).

As of pandas 0.24, there is a new `Int64` type (notice the capitalization). This is not the default integer type, but you can coerce to this type and have support for missing numbers.

The pandas-profiling library includes a profile report. You can generate this report in a notebook. It will summarize the types of the columns and allow you to view details of quantile statistics, descriptive statistics, a histogram, common values, and extreme values (see Figures 3-2 and 3-3):

```
>>> import pandas_profiling
>>> pandas_profiling.ProfileReport(df)
```

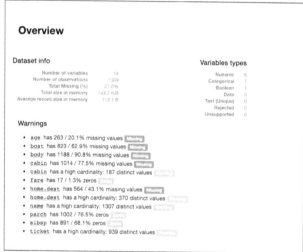

Figure 3-2. Pandas-profiling summary.

Variables

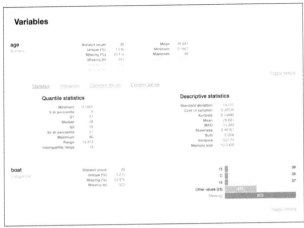

Figure 3-3. Pandas-profiling variable details.

Use the `.shape` attribute of the DataFrame to inspect the number of rows and columns:

```
>>> df.shape
(1309, 14)
```

Use the `.describe` method to get summary stats as well as see the count of nonnull data. The default behavior of this method is to only report on numeric columns. Here the output is truncated to only show the first two columns:

```
>>> df.describe().iloc[:, :2]
              pclass      survived
count   1309.000000   1309.000000
mean       2.294882      0.381971
std        0.837836      0.486055
min        1.000000      0.000000
25%        2.000000      0.000000
50%        3.000000      0.000000
75%        3.000000      1.000000
max        3.000000      1.000000
```

The count statistic only includes values that are not NaN, so it is useful for checking whether a column is missing data. It is also a good idea to spot-check the minimum and maximum values to see if there are outliers. Summary statistics are one way to do this. Plotting a histogram or a box plot is a visual representation that we will see later.

We will need to deal with missing data. Use the .isnull method to find columns or rows with missing values. Calling .isnull on a DataFrame returns a new DataFrame with every cell containing a True or False value. In Python, these values evaluate to 1 and 0, respectively. This allows us to sum them up or even calculate the percent missing (by calculating the mean).

The code indicates the count of missing data in each column:

```
>>> df.isnull().sum()
pclass         0
survived       0
name           0
sex            0
age          263
sibsp          0
parch          0
ticket         0
fare           1
cabin       1014
embarked       2
boat         823
body        1188
home.dest    564
dtype: int64
```

Replace `.sum` with `.mean` to get the percentage of null values. By default, calling these methods will apply the operation along axis 0, which is along the index. If you want to get the counts of missing features for each sample, you can apply this along axis 1 (along the columns):

```
>>> df.isnull().sum(axis=1).loc[:10]
0    1
1    1
2    2
3    1
4    2
5    1
6    1
7    2
8    1
9    2
dtype: int64
```

A SME can help in determining what to do with missing data. The age column might be useful, so keeping it and interpolating values could provide some signal to the model. Columns where most of the values are missing (cabin, boat, and body) tend to not provide value and can be dropped.

The body column (body identification number) is missing for many rows. We should drop this column at any rate because it leaks data. This column indicates that the passenger did not survive; by necessity our model could use that to cheat. We will pull it out. (If we are creating a model to predict if a passenger would die, knowing that they had a body identification number a priori would let us know they were already dead. We want our model to not know that information and make the prediction based on the other columns.) Likewise, the boat column leaks the reverse information (that a passenger survived).

Let's look at some of the rows with missing data. We can create a boolean array (a series with True or False to indicate if the row has missing data) and use it to inspect rows that are missing data:

```
>>> mask = df.isnull().any(axis=1)

>>> mask.head()  # rows
0    True
1    True
2    True
3    True
4    True
dtype: bool

>>> df[mask].body.head()
0      NaN
1      NaN
2      NaN
3    135.0
4      NaN
Name: body, dtype: float64
```

We will impute (or derive values for) the missing values for the age column later.

Columns with type of object tend to be categorical (but they may also be high cardinality string data, or a mix of column types). For object columns that we believe to be categorical, use the .value_counts method to examine the counts of the values:

```
>>> df.sex.value_counts(dropna=False)
male      843
female    466
Name: sex, dtype: int64
```

Remember that pandas typically ignores null or NaN values. If you want to include those, use dropna=False to also show counts for NaN:

```
>>> df.embarked.value_counts(dropna=False)
S      914
C      270
Q      123
NaN      2
Name: embarked, dtype: int64
```

We have a couple of options for dealing with missing embarked values. Using S might seem logical as that is the most common value. We could dig into the data and try and determine if another option is better. We could also drop those two values. Or, because this is categorical, we can ignore them and use pandas to create dummy columns if these two samples will just have 0 entries for every option. We will use this latter choice for this feature.

Create Features

We can drop columns that have no variance or no signal. There aren't features like that in this dataset, but if there was a column called "is human" that had 1 for every sample this column would not be providing any information.

Alternatively, unless we are using NLP or extracting data out of text columns where every value is different, a model will not be able to take advantage of this column. The name column is an example of this. Some have pulled out the title t from the name and treated it as categorical.

We also want to drop columns that leak information. Both boat and body columns leak whether a passenger survived.

The pandas .drop method can drop either rows or columns:

```
>>> name = df.name
>>> name.head(3)
0       Allen, Miss. Elisabeth Walton
1      Allison, Master. Hudson Trevor
2        Allison, Miss. Helen Loraine
Name: name, dtype: object
```

```
>>> df = df.drop(
...     columns=[
...         "name",
...         "ticket",
...         "home.dest",
...         "boat",
...         "body",
...         "cabin",
...     ]
... )
```

We need to create dummy columns from string columns. This will create new columns for sex and embarked. Pandas has a convenient get_dummies function for that:

```
>>> df = pd.get_dummies(df)

>>> df.columns
Index(['pclass', 'survived', 'age', 'sibsp',
    'parch', 'fare', 'sex_female', 'sex_male',
    'embarked_C', 'embarked_Q', 'embarked_S'],
    dtype='object')
```

At this point the sex_male and sex_female columns are perfectly inverse correlated. Typically we remove any columns with perfect or very high positive or negative correlation. Multicollinearity can impact interpretation of feature importance and coefficients in some models. Here is code to remove the sex_male column:

```
>>> df = df.drop(columns="sex_male")
```

Alternatively, we can add a drop_first=True parameter to the get_dummies call:

```
>>> df = pd.get_dummies(df, drop_first=True)

>>> df.columns
Index(['pclass', 'survived', 'age', 'sibsp',
    'parch', 'fare', 'sex_male',
    'embarked_Q', 'embarked_S'],
    dtype='object')
```

Create a DataFrame (X) with the features and a series (y) with the labels. We could also use numpy arrays, but then we don't have column names:

```
>>> y = df.survived
>>> X = df.drop(columns="survived")
```

TIP

We can use the pyjanitor library (*https://oreil.ly/_IWbA*) to replace the last two lines:

```
>>> import janitor as jn
>>> X, y = jn.get_features_targets(
...     df, target_columns="survived"
... )
```

Sample Data

We always want to train and test on different data. Otherwise you don't really know how well your model generalizes to data that it hasn't seen before. We'll use scikit-learn to pull out 30% for testing (using `random_state=42` to remove an element of randomness if we start comparing different models):

```
>>> X_train, X_test, y_train, y_test = model_selec
tion.train_test_split(
...     X, y, test_size=0.3, random_state=42
... )
```

Impute Data

The age column has missing values. We need to impute age from the numeric values. We only want to impute on the training set and then use that imputer to fill in the date for the test set. Otherwise we are leaking data (cheating by giving future information to the model).

Now that we have test and train data, we can impute missing values on the training set, and use the trained imputers to fill in the test dataset. The fancyimpute library (*https://oreil.ly/Vlf9e*) has many algorithms that it implements. Sadly, most of these algorithms are not implemented in an *inductive* manner. This means that you cannot call .fit and then .transform, which means you cannot impute for new data based on how the model was trained.

The IterativeImputer class (which was in fancyimpute but has been migrated to scikit-learn) does support inductive mode. To use it we need to add a special experimental import (as of scikit-learn version 0.21.2):

```
>>> from sklearn.experimental import (
...     enable_iterative_imputer,
... )
>>> from sklearn import impute
>>> num_cols = [
...     "pclass",
...     "age",
...     "sibsp",
...     "parch",
...     "fare",
...     "sex_female",
... ]

>>> imputer = impute.IterativeImputer()
>>> imputed = imputer.fit_transform(
...     X_train[num_cols]
... )
>>> X_train.loc[:, num_cols] = imputed
>>> imputed = imputer.transform(X_test[num_cols])
>>> X_test.loc[:, num_cols] = imputed
```

If we wanted to impute with the median, we can use pandas to do that:

```
>>> meds = X_train.median()
>>> X_train = X_train.fillna(meds)
>>> X_test = X_test.fillna(meds)
```

Normalize Data

Normalizing or preprocessing the data will help many models perform better after this is done. Particularly those that depend on a distance metric to determine similarity. (Note that tree models, which treat each feature on its own, don't have this requirement.)

We are going to standardize the data for the preprocessing. Standardizing is translating the data so that it has a mean value of zero and a standard deviation of one. This way models don't treat variables with larger scales as more important than smaller scaled variables. I'm going to stick the result (numpy array) back into a pandas DataFrame for easier manipulation (and to keep column names).

I also normally don't standardize dummy columns, so I will ignore those:

```
>>> cols = "pclass,age,sibsp,fare".split(",")
>>> sca = preprocessing.StandardScaler()
>>> X_train = sca.fit_transform(X_train)
>>> X_train = pd.DataFrame(X_train, columns=cols)
>>> X_test = sca.transform(X_test)
>>> X_test = pd.DataFrame(X_test, columns=cols)
```

Refactor

At this point I like to refactor my code. I typically make two functions. One for general cleaning, and another for dividing up into a training and testing set and to perform mutations that need to happen differently on those sets:

```
>>> def tweak_titanic(df):
...     df = df.drop(
...         columns=[
...             "name",
...             "ticket",
...             "home.dest",
...             "boat",
...             "body",
```

```
...                "cabin",
...            ]
...        ).pipe(pd.get_dummies, drop_first=True)
...        return df

>>> def get_train_test_X_y(
...     df, y_col, size=0.3, std_cols=None
... ):
...     y = df[y_col]
...     X = df.drop(columns=y_col)
...     X_train, X_test, y_train, y_test =
model_selection.train_test_split(
...         X, y, test_size=size, random_state=42
...     )
...     cols = X.columns
...     num_cols = [
...         "pclass",
...         "age",
...         "sibsp",
...         "parch",
...         "fare",
...     ]
...     fi = impute.IterativeImputer()
...     X_train.loc[
...         :, num_cols
...     ] = fi.fit_transform(X_train[num_cols])
...     X_test.loc[:, num_cols] = fi.transform(
...         X_test[num_cols]
...     )
...
...     if std_cols:
...         std = preprocessing.StandardScaler()
...         X_train.loc[
...             :, std_cols
...         ] = std.fit_transform(
...             X_train[std_cols]
...         )
...         X_test.loc[
...             :, std_cols
...         ] = std.transform(X_test[std_cols])
```

```
...
...        return X_train, X_test, y_train, y_test

>>> ti_df = tweak_titanic(orig_df)
>>> std_cols = "pclass,age,sibsp,fare".split(",")
>>> X_train, X_test, y_train, y_test =
get_train_test_X_y(
...        ti_df, "survived", std_cols=std_cols
... )
```

Baseline Model

Creating a baseline model that does something really simple
can give us something to compare our model to. Note that
using the default .score result gives us the accuracy which can
be misleading. A problem where a positive case is 1 in 10,000
can easily get over 99% accuracy by always predicting negative.

```
>>> from sklearn.dummy import DummyClassifier
>>> bm = DummyClassifier()
>>> bm.fit(X_train, y_train)
>>> bm.score(X_test, y_test)  # accuracy
0.5292620865139949

>>> from sklearn import metrics
>>> metrics.precision_score(
...        y_test, bm.predict(X_test)
... )
0.40277777777777778
```

Various Families

This code tries a variety of algorithm families. The "No Free
Lunch" theorem states that no algorithm performs well on all
data. However, for some finite set of data, there may be an algorithm that does well on that set. (A popular choice for structured learning these days is a tree-boosted algorithm such as
XGBoost.)

Here we use a few different families and compare the AUC score and standard deviation using k-fold cross-validation. An algorithm that has a slightly smaller average score but tighter standard deviation might be a better choice.

Because we are using k-fold cross-validation, we will feed the model all of X and y:

```
>>> X = pd.concat([X_train, X_test])
>>> y = pd.concat([y_train, y_test])
>>> from sklearn import model_selection
>>> from sklearn.dummy import DummyClassifier
>>> from sklearn.linear_model import (
...     LogisticRegression,
... )
>>> from sklearn.tree import DecisionTreeClassifier
>>> from sklearn.neighbors import (
...     KNeighborsClassifier,
... )
>>> from sklearn.naive_bayes import GaussianNB
>>> from sklearn.svm import SVC
>>> from sklearn.ensemble import (
...     RandomForestClassifier,
... )
>>> import xgboost

>>> for model in [
...     DummyClassifier,
...     LogisticRegression,
...     DecisionTreeClassifier,
...     KNeighborsClassifier,
...     GaussianNB,
...     SVC,
...     RandomForestClassifier,
...     xgboost.XGBClassifier,
... ]:
...     cls = model()
...     kfold = model_selection.KFold(
...         n_splits=10, random_state=42
...     )
...     s = model_selection.cross_val_score(
```

```
...            cls, X, y, scoring="roc_auc", cv=kfold
...        )
...        print(
...            f"{model.__name__:22}  AUC: "
...            f"{s.mean():.3f} STD: {s.std():.2f}"
...        )
DummyClassifier        AUC: 0.511  STD: 0.04
LogisticRegression     AUC: 0.843  STD: 0.03
DecisionTreeClassifier AUC: 0.761  STD: 0.03
KNeighborsClassifier   AUC: 0.829  STD: 0.05
GaussianNB             AUC: 0.818  STD: 0.04
SVC                    AUC: 0.838  STD: 0.05
RandomForestClassifier AUC: 0.829  STD: 0.04
XGBClassifier          AUC: 0.864  STD: 0.04
```

Stacking

If you were going down the Kaggle route (or want maximum performance at the cost of interpretability), *stacking* is an option. A stacking classifier takes other models and uses their output to predict a target or label. We will use the previous models' outputs and combine them to see if a stacking classifier can do better:

```
>>> from mlxtend.classifier import (
...     StackingClassifier,
... )
>>> clfs = [
...     x()
...     for x in [
...         LogisticRegression,
...         DecisionTreeClassifier,
...         KNeighborsClassifier,
...         GaussianNB,
...         SVC,
...         RandomForestClassifier,
...     ]
... ]
>>> stack = StackingClassifier(
...     classifiers=clfs,
```

```
...         meta_classifier=LogisticRegression(),
... )
>>> kfold = model_selection.KFold(
...        n_splits=10, random_state=42
... )
>>> s = model_selection.cross_val_score(
...        stack, X, y, scoring="roc_auc", cv=kfold
... )
>>> print(
...        f"{stack.__class__.__name__}  "
...        f"AUC: {s.mean():.3f}  STD: {s.std():.2f}"
... )
StackingClassifier  AUC: 0.804  STD: 0.06
```

In this case it looks like performance went down a bit, as well as standard deviation.

Create Model

I'm going to use a random forest classifier to create a model. It is a flexible model that tends to give decent out-of-the-box results. Remember to train it (calling .fit) with the training data from the data that we split earlier into a training and testing set:

```
>>> rf = ensemble.RandomForestClassifier(
...        n_estimators=100, random_state=42
... )
>>> rf.fit(X_train, y_train)
RandomForestClassifier(bootstrap=True,
    class_weight=None, criterion='gini',
    max_depth=None, max_features='auto',
    max_leaf_nodes=None,
    min_impurity_decrease=0.0,
    min_impurity_split=None,
    min_samples_leaf=1, min_samples_split=2,
    min_weight_fraction_leaf=0.0, n_estimators=10,
    n_jobs=1, oob_score=False, random_state=42,
    verbose=0, warm_start=False)
```

Evaluate Model

Now that we have a model, we can use the test data to see how well the model generalizes to data that it hasn't seen before. The `.score` method of a classifier returns the average of the prediction accuracy. We want to make sure that we call the `.score` method with the test data (presumably it should perform better with the training data):

```
>>> rf.score(X_test, y_test)
0.7964376590330788
```

We can also look at other metrics, such as precision:

```
>>> metrics.precision_score(
...     y_test, rf.predict(X_test)
... )
0.8013698630136986
```

A nice benefit of tree-based models is that you can inspect the feature importance. The feature importance tells you how much a feature contributes to the model. Note that removing a feature doesn't mean that the score will go down accordingly, as other features might be colinear (in this case we could remove either the sex_male or sex_female column as they have a perfect negative correlation):

```
>>> for col, val in sorted(
...     zip(
...         X_train.columns,
...         rf.feature_importances_,
...     ),
...     key=lambda x: x[1],
...     reverse=True,
... )[:5]:
...     print(f"{col:10}{val:10.3f}")
age          0.277
fare         0.265
sex_female   0.240
pclass       0.092
sibsp        0.048
```

The feature importance is calculated by looking at the error increase. If removing a feature increases the error in the model, the feature is more important.

I really like the SHAP library for exploring what features a model deems important, and for explaining predictions. This library works with black-box models, and we will show it later.

Optimize Model

Models have *hyperparameters* that control how they behave. By varying the values for these parameters, we change their performance. Sklearn has a grid search class to evaluate a model with different combinations of parameters and return the best result. We can use those parameters to instantiate the model class:

```
>>> rf4 = ensemble.RandomForestClassifier()
>>> params = {
...     "max_features": [0.4, "auto"],
...     "n_estimators": [15, 200],
...     "min_samples_leaf": [1, 0.1],
...     "random_state": [42],
... }
>>> cv = model_selection.GridSearchCV(
...     rf4, params, n_jobs=-1
... ).fit(X_train, y_train)
>>> print(cv.best_params_)
{'max_features': 'auto', 'min_samples_leaf': 0.1,
 'n_estimators': 200, 'random_state': 42}

>>> rf5 = ensemble.RandomForestClassifier(
...     **{
...         "max_features": "auto",
...         "min_samples_leaf": 0.1,
...         "n_estimators": 200,
...         "random_state": 42,
...     }
... )
>>> rf5.fit(X_train, y_train)
```

```
>>> rf5.score(X_test, y_test)
0.7888040712468194
```

We can pass in a scoring parameter to GridSearchCV to optimize for different metrics. See Chapter 12 for a list of metrics
and their meanings.

Confusion Matrix

A confusion matrix allows us to see the correct classifications
as well as false positives and false negatives. It may be that we
want to optimize toward false positives or false negatives, and
different models or parameters can alter that. We can use
sklearn to get a text version, or Yellowbrick for a plot (see
Figure 3-4):

```
>>> from sklearn.metrics import confusion_matrix
>>> y_pred = rf5.predict(X_test)
>>> confusion_matrix(y_test, y_pred)
array([[196,  28],
       [ 55, 114]])

>>> mapping = {0: "died", 1: "survived"}
>>> fig, ax = plt.subplots(figsize=(6, 6))
>>> cm_viz = ConfusionMatrix(
...     rf5,
...     classes=["died", "survived"],
...     label_encoder=mapping,
... )
>>> cm_viz.score(X_test, y_test)
>>> cm_viz.poof()
>>> fig.savefig(
...     "images/mlpr_0304.png",
...     dpi=300,
...     bbox_inches="tight",
... )
```

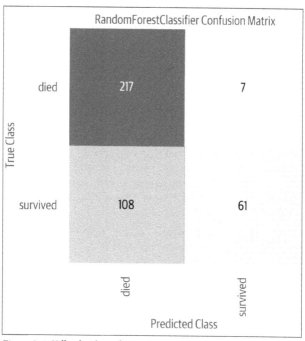

Figure 3-4. Yellowbrick confusion matrix. This is a useful evaluation tool that presents the predicted class along the bottom and the true class along the side. A good classifier would have all of the values along the diagonal, and zeros in the other cells.

ROC Curve

A receiver operating characteristic (ROC) plot is a common tool used to evaluate classifiers. By measuring the area under the curve (AUC), we can get a metric to compare different classifiers (see Figure 3-5). It plots the true positive rate against the false positive rate. We can use sklearn to calculate the AUC:

```
>>> y_pred = rf5.predict(X_test)
>>> roc_auc_score(y_test, y_pred)
0.7747781065088757
```

Or Yellowbrick to visualize the plot:

```
>>> fig, ax = plt.subplots(figsize=(6, 6))
>>> roc_viz = ROCAUC(rf5)
>>> roc_viz.score(X_test, y_test)
0.8279691030696217
>>> roc_viz.poof()
>>> fig.savefig("images/mlpr_0305.png")
```

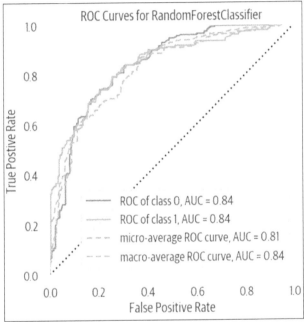

Figure 3-5. ROC curve. This shows the true positive rate against the false positive rate. In general, the further it bulges out the better. Measuring the AUC gives a single number to evaluate. Closer to one is better. Below .5 is a poor model.

Learning Curve

A learning curve is used to tell us if we have enough training data. It trains the model with increasing portions of the data and measures the score (see Figure 3-6). If the cross-validation score continues to climb, then we might need to invest in gathering more data. Here is a Yellowbrick example:

```
>>> import numpy as np
>>> fig, ax = plt.subplots(figsize=(6, 4))
>>> cv = StratifiedKFold(12)
>>> sizes = np.linspace(0.3, 1.0, 10)
>>> lc_viz = LearningCurve(
...      rf5,
...      cv=cv,
...      train_sizes=sizes,
...      scoring="f1_weighted",
...      n_jobs=4,
...      ax=ax,
... )
>>> lc_viz.fit(X, y)
>>> lc_viz.poof()
>>> fig.savefig("images/mlpr_0306.png")
```

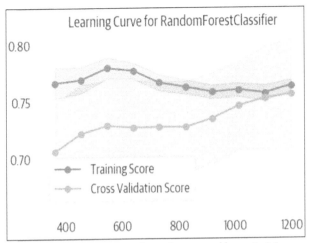

Figure 3-6. This learning curve shows that as we add more training samples, our cross-validation (testing) scores appear to improve.

Deploy Model

Using Python's `pickle` module, we can persist models and load them. Once we have a model, we call the `.predict` method to get a classification or regression result:

```
>>> import pickle
>>> pic = pickle.dumps(rf5)
>>> rf6 = pickle.loads(pic)
>>> y_pred = rf6.predict(X_test)
>>> roc_auc_score(y_test, y_pred)
0.7747781065088757
```

Using Flask (*https://palletsprojects.com/p/flask*) to deploy a web service for prediction is very common. There are now other commercial and open source products coming out that support deployment. Among them are Clipper (*http://clipper.ai/*), Pipeline (*https://oreil.ly/UfHdP*), and Google's Cloud Machine Learning Engine (*https://oreil.ly/1qYkH*).

CHAPTER 4

Missing Data

We need to deal with missing data. The previous chapter showed an example. This chapter will dive into it a bit more. Most algorithms will not work if data is missing. Notable exceptions are the recent boosting libraries: XGBoost, Cat-Boost, and LightGBM.

As with many things in machine learning, there are no hard answers for how to treat missing data. Also, missing data could represent different situations. Imagine census data coming back and an age feature being reported as missing. Is it because the sample didn't want to reveal their age? They didn't know their age? The one asking the questions forgot to even ask about age? Is there a pattern to missing ages? Does it correlate to another feature? Is it completely random?

There are also various ways to handle missing data:

- Remove any row with missing data
- Remove any column with missing data
- Impute missing values
- Create an indicator column to signify data was missing

Examining Missing Data

Let's go back to the Titanic data. Because Python treats `True` and `False` as 1 and 0, respectively, we can use this trick in pandas to get percent of missing data:

```
>>> df.isnull().mean() * 100
pclass        0.000000
survived      0.000000
name          0.000000
sex           0.000000
age          20.091673
sibsp         0.000000
parch         0.000000
ticket        0.000000
fare          0.076394
cabin        77.463713
embarked      0.152788
boat         62.872422
body         90.756303
home.dest    43.086325
dtype: float64
```

To visualize patterns in the missing data, use the missingno library (*https://oreil.ly/rgYJG*). This library is useful for viewing contiguous areas of missing data, which would indicate that the missing data is not random (see Figure 4-1). The matrix function includes a sparkline along the right side. Patterns here would also indicate nonrandom missing data. You may need to limit the number of samples to be able to see the patterns:

```
>>> import missingno as msno
>>> ax = msno.matrix(orig_df.sample(500))
>>> ax.get_figure().savefig("images/mlpr_0401.png")
```

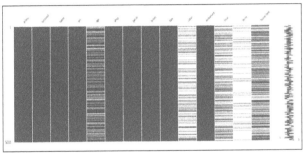

Figure 4-1. Where data is missing. No clear patterns jump out to the author.

We can create a bar plot of missing data counts using pandas
(see Figure 4-2):

```
>>> fig, ax = plt.subplots(figsize=(6, 4))
>>> (1 - df.isnull().mean()).abs().plot.bar(ax=ax)
>>> fig.savefig("images/mlpr_0402.png", dpi=300)
```

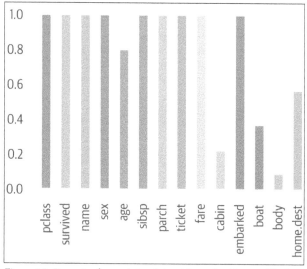

*Figure 4-2. Percents of nonmissing data with pandas. Boat and body
are leaky so we should ignore those. Interesting that some ages are
missing.*

Or use the missingno library to create the same plot (see Figure 4-3):

```
>>> ax = msno.bar(orig_df.sample(500))
>>> ax.get_figure().savefig("images/mlpr_0403.png")
```

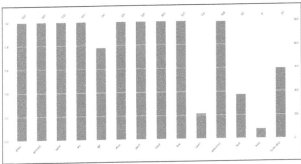

Figure 4-3. Percents of nonmissing data with missingno.

We can create a heat map showing if there are correlations where data is missing (see Figure 4-4). In this case, it doesn't look like the locations where data are missing are correlated:

```
>>> ax = msno.heatmap(df, figsize=(6, 6))
>>> ax.get_figure().savefig("/tmp/mlpr_0404.png")
```

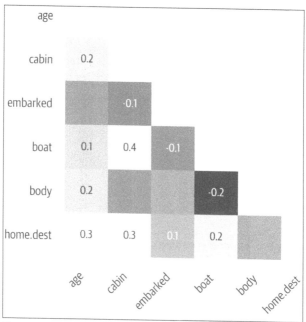

Figure 4-4. Correlations of missing data with missingno.

We can create a dendrogram showing the clusterings of where data is missing (see Figure 4-5). Leaves that are at the same level predict one another's presence (empty or filled). The vertical arms are used to indicate how different clusters are. Short arms mean that branches are similar:

```
>>> ax = msno.dendrogram(df)
>>> ax.get_figure().savefig("images/mlpr_0405.png")
```

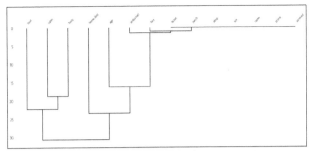

Figure 4-5. Dendrogram of missing data with missingno. We can see the columns without missing data on the upper right.

Dropping Missing Data

The pandas library can drop all rows with missing data with the `.dropna` method:

```
>>> df1 = df.dropna()
```

To drop columns, we can note what columns are missing and use the `.drop` method. We can pass in a list of column names or a single column name:

```
>>> df1 = df.drop(columns="cabin")
```

Alternatively, we can use the `.dropna` method and set `axis=1` (drop along the column axis):

```
>>> df1 = df.dropna(axis=1)
```

Be careful about dropping data. I typically view this as a last resort option.

Imputing Data

Once you have a tool for predicting data, you can use that to predict missing data. The general task of defining values for missing values is called *imputation*.

If you are imputing data, you will need to build up a pipeline and use the same imputation logic during model creation and prediction time. The `SimpleImputer` class in scikit-learn will handle mean, median, and most frequent feature values.

The default behavior is to calculate the mean:

```
>>> from sklearn.impute import SimpleImputer
>>> num_cols = df.select_dtypes(
...     include="number"
... ).columns
>>> im = SimpleImputer()  # mean
>>> imputed = im.fit_transform(df[num_cols])
```

Provide `strategy='median'` or `strategy='most_frequent'` to change the replaced value to median or most common, respectively. If you wish to fill with a constant value, say -1, use `strategy='constant'` in combination with `fill_value=-1`.

TIP

You can use the `.fillna` method in pandas to impute missing values as well. Make sure that you do not leak data though. If you are filling in with the mean value, make sure you use the same mean value during model creation and model prediction time.

The most frequent and constant strategies may be used with numeric or string data. The mean and median require numeric data.

The fancyimpute library implements many algorithms and follows the scikit-learn interface. Sadly, most of the algorithms are *transductive*, meaning that you can't call the `.transform` method by itself after fitting the algorithm. The `IterativeIm puter` is *inductive* (has since been migrated from fancyimpute to scikit-learn) and supports transforming after fitting.

Adding Indicator Columns

The lack of data in and of itself may provide some signal to a model. The pandas library can add a new column to indicate that a value was missing:

```
>>> def add_indicator(col):
...     def wrapper(df):
...         return df[col].isna().astype(int)
...
...     return wrapper

>>> df1 = df.assign(
...     cabin_missing=add_indicator("cabin")
... )
```

CHAPTER 5

Cleaning Data

We can use generic tools like pandas and specialized tools like pyjanitor to help with cleaning data.

Column Names

When using pandas, having Python-friendly column names makes attribute access possible. The pyjanitor `clean_names` function will return a DataFrame with columns in lowercase and spaces replaced by underscores:

```
>>> import janitor as jn
>>> Xbad = pd.DataFrame(
...     {
...         "A": [1, None, 3],
...         " sales numbers ": [20.0, 30.0, None],
...     }
... )
>>> jn.clean_names(Xbad)
     a  _sales_numbers_
0  1.0             20.0
1  NaN             30.0
2  3.0              NaN
```

I recommend updating columns using index assignment, the .assign method, .loc or .iloc assignment. I also recommend not using attribute assignment to update columns in pandas. Due to the risk of overwriting existing methods with the same name as a column, attribute assignment is not guaranteed to work.

The pyjanitor library is handy, but doesn't allow us to strip whitespace around columns. We can use pandas to have more fine-grained control of the column renaming:

```
>>> def clean_col(name):
...     return (
...         name.strip().lower().replace(" ", "_")
...     )

>>> Xbad.rename(columns=clean_col)
     a  sales_numbers
0  1.0           20.0
1  NaN           30.0
2  3.0            NaN
```

Replacing Missing Values

The coalesce function in pyjanitor takes a DataFrame and a list of columns to consider. This is similar to functionality found in Excel and SQL databases. It returns the first nonnull value for each row:

```
>>> jn.coalesce(
...     Xbad,
...     columns=["A", " sales numbers "],
...     new_column_name="val",
... )
    val
0   1.0
```

```
1   30.0
2   3.0
```

If we want to fill missing values with a particular value, we can use the DataFrame `.fillna` method:

```
>>> Xbad.fillna(10)
      A    sales numbers
0   1.0             20.0
1  10.0             30.0
2   3.0             10.0
```

or the pyjanitor `fill_empty` function:

```
>>> jn.fill_empty(
...     Xbad,
...     columns=["A", " sales numbers "],
...     value=10,
... )
      A    sales numbers
0   1.0             20.0
1  10.0             30.0
2   3.0             10.0
```

Often, we will use finer-grained imputations in pandas, scikit-learn, or fancyimpute to perform per-column null replacement.

As a sanity check before creating models, you can use pandas to ensure that you have dealt with all missing values. The following code returns a single boolean if there is any cell that is missing in a DataFrame:

```
>>> df.isna().any().any()
True
```

CHAPTER 6

Exploring

It has been said that it is easier to take a SME and train them in data science than the reverse. I'm not sure I agree with that 100%, but there is truth that data has nuance and an SME can help tease that apart. By understanding the business and the data, they are able to create better models and have a better impact on their business.

Before I create a model, I will do some exploratory data analysis. This gives me a feel for the data, but also is a great excuse to meet and discuss issues with business units that control that data.

Data Size

Again, we are using the Titanic dataset here. The pandas `.shape` property will return a tuple of the number of rows and columns:

```
>>> X.shape
(1309, 13)
```

We can see that this dataset has 1,309 rows and 13 columns.

Summary Stats

We can use pandas to get summary statistics for our data. The `.describe` method will also give us the count of non-NaN values. Let's look at the results for the first and last columns:

```
>>> X.describe().iloc[:, [0, -1]]
            pclass    embarked_S
count  1309.000000   1309.000000
mean     -0.012831      0.698243
std       0.995822      0.459196
min      -1.551881      0.000000
25%      -0.363317      0.000000
50%       0.825248      1.000000
75%       0.825248      1.000000
max       0.825248      1.000000
```

The count row tells us that both of these columns are filled in. There are no missing values. We also have the mean, standard deviation, minimum, maximum, and quartile values.

NOTE

A pandas DataFrame has an `iloc` attribute that we can do index operations on. It will let us pick out rows and columns by index location. We pass in the row positions as a scalar, list, or slice, and then we can add a comma and pass in the column positions as a scalar, list, or slice.

Here we pull out the second and fifth row, and the last three columns:

```
>>> X.iloc[[1, 4], -3:]
     sex_male  embarked_Q  embarked_S
677       1.0           0           1
864       0.0           0           1
```

There is also a `.loc` attribute, and we can put out rows and columns based on name (rather than position). Here is the same portion of the DataFrame:

```
>>> X.loc[[677, 864], "sex_male":]
     sex_male  embarked_Q  embarked_S
677       1.0           0           1
864       0.0           0           1
```

Histogram

A histogram is a great tool to visualize numeric data. You can see how many modes there are as well as look at the distribution (see Figure 6-1). The pandas library has a `.plot` method to show histograms:

```
>>> fig, ax = plt.subplots(figsize=(6, 4))
>>> X.fare.plot(kind="hist", ax=ax)
>>> fig.savefig("images/mlpr_0601.png", dpi=300)
```

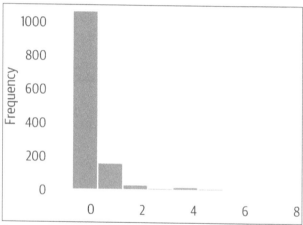

Figure 6-1. Pandas histogram.

Using the seaborn library, we can plot a histogram of continuous values against the target (see Figure 6-2):

```
fig, ax = plt.subplots(figsize=(12, 8))
mask = y_train == 1
ax = sns.distplot(X_train[mask].fare, label='sur
vived')
ax = sns.distplot(X_train[~mask].fare,
label='died')
ax.set_xlim(-1.5, 1.5)
ax.legend()
```

```
fig.savefig('images/mlpr_0602.png', dpi=300,
bbox_inches='tight')
```

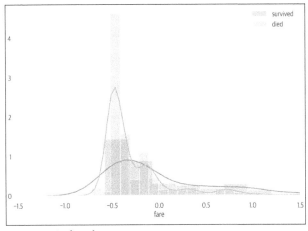

Figure 6-2. Seaborn histogram.

Scatter Plot

A scatter plot shows the relationship between two numeric columns (see Figure 6-3). Again, this is easy with pandas. Adjust the alpha parameter if you have overlapping data:

```
>>> fig, ax = plt.subplots(figsize=(6, 4))
>>> X.plot.scatter(
...     x="age", y="fare", ax=ax, alpha=0.3
... )
>>> fig.savefig("images/mlpr_0603.png", dpi=300)
```

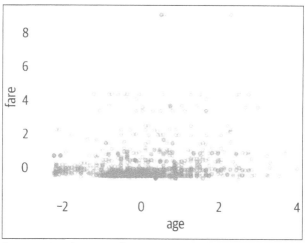

Figure 6-3. Pandas scatter plot.

There doesn't appear to be much correlation between these two features. We can do Pearson correlation between two (pandas) columns with the .corr method to quantify the correlation:

```
>>> X.age.corr(X.fare)
0.17818151568062093
```

Joint Plot

Yellowbrick has a fancier scatter plot that includes histograms on the edge as well as a regression line called a *joint plot* (see Figure 6-4):

```
>>> from yellowbrick.features import (
...     JointPlotVisualizer,
... )
>>> fig, ax = plt.subplots(figsize=(6, 6))
>>> jpv = JointPlotVisualizer(
...     feature="age", target="fare"
... )
>>> jpv.fit(X["age"], X["fare"])
```

```
>>> jpv.poof()
>>> fig.savefig("images/mlpr_0604.png", dpi=300)
```

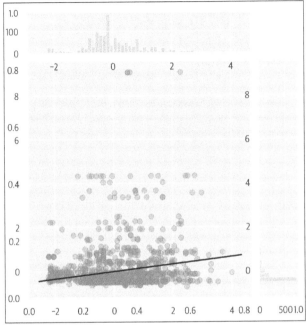

Figure 6-4. Yellowbrick joint plot.

WARNING

In this `.fit` method, X and y refer to a column each. Usually, the X is a DataFrame, not a series.

You can also use the seaborn (*https://seaborn.pydata.org*) library to create a joint plot (see Figure 6-5):

```
>>> from seaborn import jointplot
>>> fig, ax = plt.subplots(figsize=(6, 6))
>>> new_df = X.copy()
>>> new_df["target"] = y
>>> p = jointplot(
...     "age", "fare", data=new_df, kind="reg"
... )
>>> p.savefig("images/mlpr_0605.png", dpi=300)
```

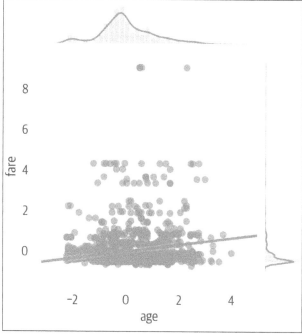

Figure 6-5. Seaborn joint plot.

Pair Grid

The seaborn library can create a pair grid (see Figure 6-6). This plot is a matrix of columns and kernel density estimations. To color by a column from a DataFrame, use the hue parameter. By coloring with the target, we can see if features have different effects on the target:

```
>>> from seaborn import pairplot
>>> fig, ax = plt.subplots(figsize=(6, 6))
>>> new_df = X.copy()
>>> new_df["target"] = y
>>> vars = ["pclass", "age", "fare"]
>>> p = pairplot(
...     new_df, vars=vars, hue="target", kind="reg"
... )
>>> p.savefig("images/mlpr_0606.png", dpi=300)
```

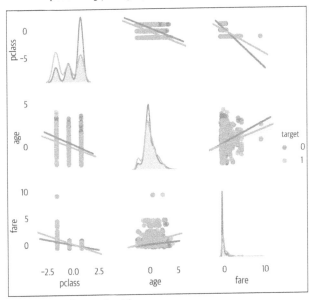

Figure 6-6. Seaborn pair grid.

Box and Violin Plots

Seaborn has various plots to visualize distributions. We show examples of a box plot and a violin plot (see Figure 6-7 and Figure 6-8). These plots can visualize a feature against a target:

```
>>> from seaborn import box plot
>>> fig, ax = plt.subplots(figsize=(8, 6))
>>> new_df = X.copy()
>>> new_df["target"] = y
>>> boxplot(x="target", y="age", data=new_df)
>>> fig.savefig("images/mlpr_0607.png", dpi=300)
```

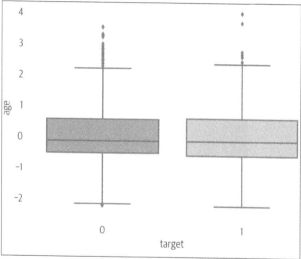

Figure 6-7. Seaborn box plot.

Violin plots can help with distribution visualization:

```
>>> from seaborn import violinplot
>>> fig, ax = plt.subplots(figsize=(8, 6))
>>> new_df = X.copy()
>>> new_df["target"] = y
>>> violinplot(
...         x="target", y="sex_male", data=new_df
```

```
... )
>>> fig.savefig("images/mlpr_0608.png", dpi=300)
```

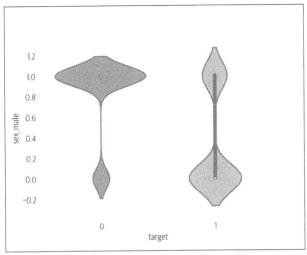

Figure 6-8. Seaborn violin plot.

Comparing Two Ordinal Values

Here is pandas code to compare two ordinal categories. I'm
simulating that by binning age into ten quantiles, and pclass
into three bins. The plot is normalized so it fills all of the vertical area. This makes it easy to see that in the 40% quantile most
of the tickets were in 3rd class (see Figure 6-9):

```
>>> fig, ax = plt.subplots(figsize=(8, 6))
>>> (
...       X.assign(
...           age_bin=pd.qcut(
...               X.age, q=10, labels=False
...           ),
...           class_bin=pd.cut(
...               X.pclass, bins=3, labels=False
...           ),
```

```
...          )
...          .groupby(["age_bin", "class_bin"])
...          .size()
...          .unstack()
...          .pipe(lambda df: df.div(df.sum(1), axis=0))
...          .plot.bar(
...              stacked=True,
...              width=1,
...              ax=ax,
...              cmap="viridis",
...          )
...          .legend(bbox_to_anchor=(1, 1))
... )
>>> fig.savefig(
...      "image/mlpr_0609.png",
...      dpi=300,
...      bbox_inches="tight",
... )
```

NOTE

The lines:

```
.groupby(["age_bin", "class_bin"])
.size()
.unstack()
```

can be replaced by:

```
.pipe(lambda df: pd.crosstab(
    df.age_bin, df.class_bin)
)
```

In pandas, there is often more than one way to do something, and some helper functions are available that compose other functionality, such as pd.crosstab.

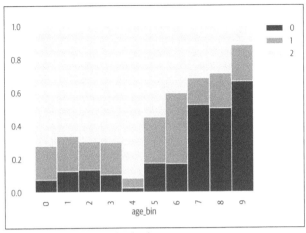

Figure 6-9. Comparing ordinal values.

Correlation

Yellowbrick can create pairwise comparisons between the features (see Figure 6-10). This plot shows a Pearson correlation (the `algorithm` parameter also accepts `'spearman'` and `'covariance'`):

```
>>> from yellowbrick.features import Rank2D
>>> fig, ax = plt.subplots(figsize=(6, 6))
>>> pcv = Rank2D(
...     features=X.columns, algorithm="pearson"
... )
>>> pcv.fit(X, y)
>>> pcv.transform(X)
>>> pcv.poof()
>>> fig.savefig(
...     "images/mlpr_0610.png",
...     dpi=300,
...     bbox_inches="tight",
... )
```

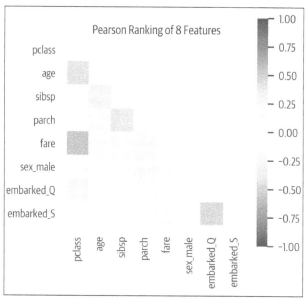

Figure 6-10. Covariance correlation created with Yellowbrick.

A similar plot, a heat map, is available in the seaborn library (see Figure 6-11). We need to pass in a correlation DataFrame as the data. Sadly, the colorbar does not span between -1 and 1 unless the values in the matrix do, or we add the vmin and vmax parameters:

```
>>> from seaborn import heatmap
>>> fig, ax = plt.subplots(figsize=(8, 8))
>>> ax = heatmap(
...     X.corr(),
...     fmt=".2f",
...     annot=True,
...     ax=ax,
...     cmap="RdBu_r",
...     vmin=-1,
...     vmax=1,
... )
```

```
>>> fig.savefig(
...     "images/mlpr_0611.png",
...     dpi=300,
...     bbox_inches="tight",
... )
```

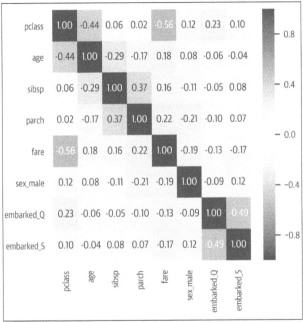

Figure 6-11. Seaborn heat map.

The pandas library can also provide a correlation between DataFrame columns. We only show the first two columns of the result. The default method is `'pearson'`, but you can also set the method parameter to `'kendall'`, `'spearman'`, or a custom callable that returns a float given two columns:

```
>>> X.corr().iloc[:, :2]
            pclass       age
pclass    1.000000 -0.440769
age      -0.440769  1.000000
```

```
sibsp        0.060832 -0.292051
parch        0.018322 -0.174992
fare        -0.558831  0.177205
sex_male     0.124617  0.077636
embarked_Q   0.230491 -0.061146
embarked_S   0.096335 -0.041315
```

Highly correlated columns don't add value and can throw off feature importance and interpretation of regression coefficients. Below is code to find the correlated columns. In our data none of the columns are highly correlated (remember we removed the sex_male column).

If we had correlated columns, we could choose to remove either the columns from level_0 or level_1 from the feature data:

```
>>> def correlated_columns(df, threshold=0.95):
...     return (
...         df.corr()
...         .pipe(
...             lambda df1: pd.DataFrame(
...                 np.tril(df1, k=-1),
...                 columns=df.columns,
...                 index=df.columns,
...             )
...         )
...         .stack()
...         .rename("pearson")
...         .pipe(
...             lambda s: s[
...                 s.abs() > threshold
...             ].reset_index()
...         )
...         .query("level_0 not in level_1")
...     )

>>> correlated_columns(X)
Empty DataFrame
Columns: [level_0, level_1, pearson]
Index: []
```

Using the dataset with more columns, we can see that many of them are correlated:

```
>>> c_df = correlated_columns(agg_df)
>>> c_df.style.format({"pearson": "{:.2f}"})
        level_0       level_1   pearson
3    pclass_mean        pclass    1.00
4    pclass_mean    pclass_min    1.00
5    pclass_mean    pclass_max    1.00
6     sibsp_mean     sibsp_max    0.97
7     parch_mean    parch_min    0.95
8     parch_mean    parch_max    0.96
9      fare_mean          fare    0.95
10     fare_mean      fare_max    0.98
12     body_mean      body_min    1.00
13     body_mean      body_max    1.00
14      sex_male    sex_female   -1.00
15    embarked_S    embarked_C   -0.95
```

RadViz

A RadViz plot shows each sample on a circle, with the features on the circumference (see Figure 6-12). The values are normalized, and you can imagine that each figure has a spring that pulls samples to it based on the value.

This is one technique to visualize separability between the targets.

Yellowbrick can do this:

```
>>> from yellowbrick.features import RadViz
>>> fig, ax = plt.subplots(figsize=(6, 6))
>>> rv = RadViz(
...     classes=["died", "survived"],
...     features=X.columns,
... )
>>> rv.fit(X, y)
>>> _ = rv.transform(X)
>>> rv.poof()
>>> fig.savefig("images/mlpr_0612.png", dpi=300)
```

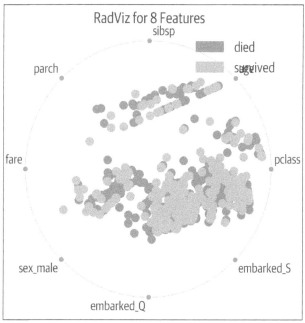

Figure 6-12. Yellowbrick RadViz plot.

The pandas library can plot RadViz plots as well (see Figure 6-13):

```
>>> from pandas.plotting import radviz
>>> fig, ax = plt.subplots(figsize=(6, 6))
>>> new_df = X.copy()
>>> new_df["target"] = y
>>> radviz(
...     new_df, "target", ax=ax, colormap="PiYG"
... )
>>> fig.savefig("images/mlpr_0613.png", dpi=300)
```

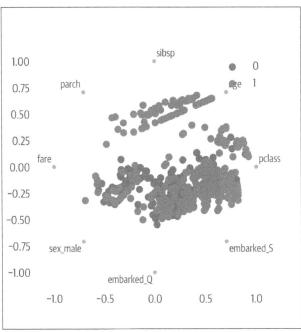

Figure 6-13. Pandas RadViz plot.

Parallel Coordinates

For multivariate data, you can use a parallel coordinates plot to see clustering visually (see Figure 6-14 and Figure 6-15).

Again, here is a Yellowbrick version:

```
>>> from yellowbrick.features import (
...      ParallelCoordinates,
... )
>>> fig, ax = plt.subplots(figsize=(6, 4))
>>> pc = ParallelCoordinates(
...      classes=["died", "survived"],
...      features=X.columns,
... )
```

```
>>> pc.fit(X, y)
>>> pc.transform(X)
>>> ax.set_xticklabels(
...     ax.get_xticklabels(), rotation=45
... )
>>> pc.poof()
>>> fig.savefig("images/mlpr_0614.png", dpi=300)
```

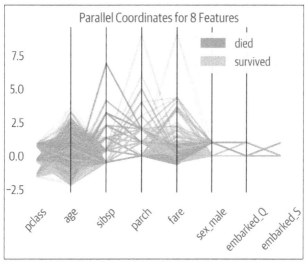

Figure 6-14. Yellowbrick parallel coordinates plot.

And a pandas version:

```
>>> from pandas.plotting import (
...     parallel_coordinates,
... )
>>> fig, ax = plt.subplots(figsize=(6, 4))
>>> new_df = X.copy()
>>> new_df["target"] = y
>>> parallel_coordinates(
...     new_df,
...     "target",
...     ax=ax,
...     colormap="viridis",
```

```
...         alpha=0.5,
... )
>>> ax.set_xticklabels(
...         ax.get_xticklabels(), rotation=45
... )
>>> fig.savefig(
...         "images/mlpr_0615.png",
...         dpi=300,
...         bbox_inches="tight",
... )
```

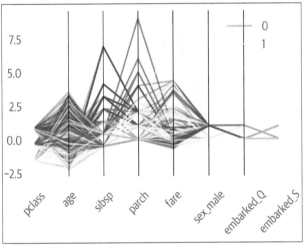

Figure 6-15. Pandas parallel coordinates plot.

CHAPTER 7

Preprocess Data

This chapter will explore common preprocessing steps using this data:

```
>>> X2 = pd.DataFrame(
...     {
...         "a": range(5),
...         "b": [-100, -50, 0, 200, 1000],
...     }
... )
>>> X2
   a     b
0  0  -100
1  1   -50
2  2     0
3  3   200
4  4  1000
```

Standardize

Some algorithms, such as SVM, perform better when the data is *standardized*. Each column should have a mean value of 0 and standard deviation of 1. Sklearn provides a .fit_transform method that combines both .fit and .transform:

```
>>> from sklearn import preprocessing
>>> std = preprocessing.StandardScaler()
```

```
>>> std.fit_transform(X2)
array([[-1.41421356, -0.75995002],
       [-0.70710678, -0.63737744],
       [ 0.        , -0.51480485],
       [ 0.70710678, -0.02451452],
       [ 1.41421356,  1.93664683]])
```

After fitting, there are various attributes we can inspect:

```
>>> std.scale_
array([   1.41421356, 407.92156109])
>>> std.mean_
array([  2., 210.])
>>> std.var_
array([2.000e+00, 1.664e+05])
```

Here is a pandas version. Remember that you will need to track the original mean and standard deviation if you use this for preprocessing. Any sample that you will use to predict later will need to be standardized with those same values:

```
>>> X_std = (X2 - X2.mean()) / X2.std()
>>> X_std
          a         b
0 -1.264911 -0.679720
1 -0.632456 -0.570088
2  0.000000 -0.460455
3  0.632456 -0.021926
4  1.264911  1.732190

>>> X_std.mean()
a    4.440892e-17
b    0.000000e+00
dtype: float64

>>> X_std.std()
a    1.0
b    1.0
dtype: float64
```

The fastai library also implements this:

```
>>> X3 = X2.copy()
>>> from fastai.structured import scale_vars
>>> scale_vars(X3, mapper=None)
>>> X3.std()
a    1.118034
b    1.118034
dtype: float64
>>> X3.mean()
a    0.000000e+00
b    4.440892e-17
dtype: float64
```

Scale to Range

Scaling to range is translating data so it is between 0 and 1, inclusive. Having the data bounded may be useful. However, if you have outliers, you probably want to be careful using this:

```
>>> from sklearn import preprocessing
>>> mms = preprocessing.MinMaxScaler()
>>> mms.fit(X2)
>>> mms.transform(X2)
array([[0.     , 0.      ],
       [0.25   , 0.04545],
       [0.5    , 0.09091],
       [0.75   , 0.27273],
       [1.     , 1.      ]])
```

Here is a pandas version:

```
>>> (X2 - X2.min()) / (X2.max() - X2.min())
      a         b
0  0.00  0.000000
1  0.25  0.045455
2  0.50  0.090909
3  0.75  0.272727
4  1.00  1.000000
```

Dummy Variables

We can use pandas to create dummy variables from categorical data. This is also referred to as one-hot encoding, or indicator encoding. Dummy variables are especially useful if the data is nominal (unordered). The get_dummies function in pandas creates multiple columns for a categorical column, each with a 1 or 0 if the original column had that value:

```
>>> X_cat = pd.DataFrame(
...     {
...         "name": ["George", "Paul"],
...         "inst": ["Bass", "Guitar"],
...     }
... )
>>> X_cat
     name    inst
0  George    Bass
1    Paul  Guitar
```

Here is the pandas version. Note the drop_first option can be used to eliminate a column (one of the dummy columns is a linear combination of the other columns):

```
>>> pd.get_dummies(X_cat, drop_first=True)
   name_Paul  inst_Guitar
0          0            0
1          1            1
```

The pyjanitor library also has the ability to split columns with the expand_column function:

```
>>> X_cat2 = pd.DataFrame(
...     {
...         "A": [1, None, 3],
...         "names": [
...             "Fred,George",
...             "George",
...             "John,Paul",
...         ],
...     }
... )
```

```
>>> jn.expand_column(X_cat2, "names", sep=",")
     A         names Fred George John Paul
0  1.0   Fred,George    1      1    0    0
1  NaN        George    0      1    0    0
2  3.0     John,Paul    0      0    1    1
```

If we have high cardinality nominal data, we can use *label encoding*. This is introduced in the next section.

Label Encoder

An alternative to dummy variable encoding is label encoding. This will take categorical data and assign each value a number. It is useful for high cardinality data. This encoder imposes ordinality, which may or may not be desired. It can take up less space than one-hot encoding, and some (tree) algorithms can deal with this encoding.

The label encoder can only deal with one column at a time:

```
>>> from sklearn import preprocessing
>>> lab = preprocessing.LabelEncoder()
>>> lab.fit_transform(X_cat)
array([0,1])
```

If you have encoded values, applying the .inverse_transform method decodes them:

```
>>> lab.inverse_transform([1, 1, 0])
array(['Guitar', 'Guitar', 'Bass'], dtype=object)
```

You can also use pandas to label encode. First, you convert the column to a categorical column type, and then pull out the numeric code from it.

This code will create a new series of numeric data from a pandas series. We use the .as_ordered method to ensure that the category is ordered:

```
>>> X_cat.name.astype(
...      "category"
... ).cat.as_ordered().cat.codes + 1
0    1
```

```
1    2
dtype: int8
```

Frequency Encoding

Another option for handling high cardinality categorical data is to *frequency encode* it. This means replacing the name of the category with the count it had in the training data. We will use pandas to do this. First, we will use the pandas .value_counts method to make a mapping (a pandas series that maps strings to counts). With the mapping we can use the .map method to do the encoding:

```
>>> mapping = X_cat.name.value_counts()
>>> X_cat.name.map(mapping)
0    1
1    1
Name: name, dtype: int64
```

Make sure you store the training mapping so you can encode future data with the same data.

Pulling Categories from Strings

One way to increase the accuracy of the Titanic model is to pull out titles from the names. A quick hack to find the most common triples is to use the Counter class:

```
>>> from collections import Counter
>>> c = Counter()
>>> def triples(val):
...     for i in range(len(val)):
...         c[val[i : i + 3]] += 1
>>> df.name.apply(triples)
>>> c.most_common(10)
[(', M', 1282),
 (' Mr', 954),
 ('r. ', 830),
 ('Mr.', 757),
 ('s. ', 460),
 ('n, ', 320),
```

```
(' Mi', 283),
('iss', 261),
('ss.', 261),
('Mis', 260)]
```

We can see that "Mr." and "Miss." are very common.

Another option is to use a regular expression to pull out the capital letter followed by lowercase letters and a period:

```
>>> df.name.str.extract(
...     "([A-Za-z]+)\.", expand=False
... ).head()
0      Miss
1    Master
2      Miss
3        Mr
4       Mrs
Name: name, dtype: object
```

We can use .value_counts to see the frequency of these:

```
>>> df.name.str.extract(
...     "([A-Za-z]+)\.", expand=False
... ).value_counts()
Mr        757
Miss      260
Mrs       197
Master     61
Dr          8
Rev         8
Col         4
Mlle        2
Ms          2
Major       2
Dona        1
Don         1
Lady        1
Countess    1
Capt        1
Sir         1
Mme         1
```

```
Jonkheer       1
Name: name, dtype: int64
```

NOTE

A complete discussion of regular expressions is beyond the scope of this book. This expression captures a group with one or more alphabetic characters. This group will be followed by a period.

Using these manipulations and pandas, you can create dummy variables or combine columns with low counts into other categories (or drop them).

Other Categorical Encoding

The categorical_encoding library (*https://oreil.ly/JbxWG*) is a set of scikit-learn transformers used to convert categorical data into numeric data. A nice feature of this library is that it supports outputting pandas DataFrames (unlike scikit-learn, which transforms them into numpy arrays).

One algorithm implemented in the library is a hash encoder. This is useful if you don't know how many categories you have ahead of time or if you are using a bag of words to represent text. This will hash the categorical columns into n_components. If you are using online learning (models that can be updated), this can be very useful:

```
>>> import category_encoders as ce
>>> he = ce.HashingEncoder(verbose=1)
>>> he.fit_transform(X_cat)
   col_0  col_1  col_2  col_3  col_4  col_5
col_6  col_7
0      0      0      0      1      0      1
0      0
1      0      2      0      0      0      0
0      0
```

The ordinal encoder can convert categorical columns that have order to a single column of numbers. Here we convert the size column to ordinal numbers. If a value is missing from the mapping dictionary, the default value of -1 is used:

```
>>> size_df = pd.DataFrame(
...     {
...         "name": ["Fred", "John", "Matt"],
...         "size": ["small", "med", "xxl"],
...     }
... )
>>> ore = ce.OrdinalEncoder(
...     mapping=[
...         {
...             "col": "size",
...             "mapping": {
...                 "small": 1,
...                 "med": 2,
...                 "lg": 3,
...             },
...         }
...     ]
... )
>>> ore.fit_transform(size_df)
   name  size
0  Fred   1.0
1  John   2.0
2  Matt  -1.0
```

This reference (*https://oreil.ly/JUtYh*) explains many of the algorithms of the categorical_encoding library.

If you have high cardinality data (a large number of unique values) consider using one of the Bayesian encoders that output a single column per categorical column. These are TargetEncoder, LeaveOneOutEncoder, WOEEncoder, JamesSteinEncoder, and MEstimateEncoder.

For example, to convert the Titanic survival column to a blend of posterior probability of the target and the prior probability given the title (categorical) information, use the following code:

```
>>> def get_title(df):
...     return df.name.str.extract(
...         "([A-Za-z]+)\.", expand=False
...     )
>>> te = ce.TargetEncoder(cols="Title")
>>> te.fit_transform(
...     df.assign(Title=get_title), df.survived
... )["Title"].head()
0    0.676923
1    0.508197
2    0.676923
3    0.162483
4    0.786802
Name: Title, dtype: float64
```

Date Feature Engineering

The fastai library has an add_datepart function that will generate date attribute columns based on a datetime column. This is useful as most machine learning algorithms would not be able to infer this type of signal from a numeric representation of a date:

```
>>> from fastai.tabular.transform import (
...     add_datepart,
... )
>>> dates = pd.DataFrame(
...     {
...         "A": pd.to_datetime(
...             ["9/17/2001", "Jan 1, 2002"]
...         )
...     }
... )

>>> add_datepart(dates, "A")
>>> dates.T
                    0       1
AYear            2001    2002
AMonth              9       1
AWeek              38       1
```

ADay	17	1
ADayofweek	0	1
ADayofyear	260	1
AIs_month_end	False	False
AIs_month_start	False	True
AIs_quarter_end	False	False
AIs_quarter_start	False	True
AIs_year_end	False	False
AIs_year_start	False	True
AElapsed	1000684800	1009843200

WARNING

`add_datepart` mutates the DataFrame, which pandas can do, but normally doesn't!

Add col_na Feature

The fastai library used to have a function for creating a column to fill a missing value (with the median) and indicate that a value was missing. There might be some signal in knowing that a value was missing. Here is a copy of the function and an example using it:

```
>>> from pandas.api.types import is_numeric_dtype
>>> def fix_missing(df, col, name, na_dict):
...     if is_numeric_dtype(col):
...         if pd.isnull(col).sum() or (
...             name in na_dict
...         ):
...             df[name + "_na"] = pd.isnull(col)
...             filler = (
...                 na_dict[name]
...                 if name in na_dict
...                 else col.median()
...             )
...             df[name] = col.fillna(filler)
...             na_dict[name] = filler
```

```
...        return na_dict
>>> data = pd.DataFrame({"A": [0, None, 5, 100]})
>>> fix_missing(data, data.A, "A", {})
{'A': 5.0}
>>> data
       A    A_na
0    0.0   False
1    5.0   True
2    5.0   False
3  100.0   False
```

Here is a pandas version:

```
>>> data = pd.DataFrame({"A": [0, None, 5, 100]})
>>> data["A_na"] = data.A.isnull()
>>> data["A"] = data.A.fillna(data.A.median())
```

Manual Feature Engineering

We can use pandas to generate new features. For the Titanic
dataset, we can add aggregate cabin data (maximum age per
cabin, mean age per cabin, etc.). To get aggregate data per cabin
and merge it back in, use the pandas .groupby method to create
the data. Then align it back to the original data using
the .merge method:

```
>>> agg = (
...        df.groupby("cabin")
...        .agg("min,max,mean,sum".split(","))
...        .reset_index()
... )
>>> agg.columns = [
...        "_".join(c).strip("_")
...        for c in agg.columns.values
... ]
>>> agg_df = df.merge(agg, on="cabin")
```

If you wanted to sum up "good" or "bad" columns, you could
create a new column that is the sum of the aggregated columns
(or another mathematical operation). This is somewhat of an
art and also requires understanding the data.

CHAPTER 8

Feature Selection

We use feature selection to select features that are useful to the model. Irrelevant features may have a negative effect on a model. Correlated features can make coefficients in regression (or feature importance in tree models) unstable or difficult to interpret.

The *curse of dimensionality* is another issue to consider. As you increase the number of dimensions of your data, it becomes more sparse. This can make it difficult to pull out a signal unless you have more data. Neighbor calculations tend to lose their usefulness as more dimensions are added.

Also, training time is usually a function of the number of columns (and sometimes it is worse than linear). If you can be concise and precise with your columns, you can have a better model in less time. We will walk through some examples using the `agg_df` dataset from the last chapter. Remember that this is the Titanic dataset with some extra columns for cabin information. Because this dataset is aggregating numeric values for each cabin, it will show many correlations. Other options include PCA and looking at the `.feature_importances_` of a tree classifier.

Collinear Columns

We can use the previously defined `correlated_columns` function or run the following code to find columns that have a correlation coefficient of .95 or above:

```
>>> limit = 0.95
>>> corr = agg_df.corr()
>>> mask = np.triu(
...     np.ones(corr.shape), k=1
... ).astype(bool)
>>> corr_no_diag = corr.where(mask)
>>> coll = [
...     c
...     for c in corr_no_diag.columns
...     if any(abs(corr_no_diag[c]) > threshold)
... ]
>>> coll
['pclass_min', 'pclass_max', 'pclass_mean',
 'sibsp_mean', 'parch_mean', 'fare_mean',
 'body_max', 'body_mean', 'sex_male', 'embarked_S']
```

The Yellowbrick `Rank2` visualizer, shown previously, will plot a
heat map of correlations.

The rfpimp package (*https://oreil.ly/MsnXc*) has a visualization
of *multicollinearity*. The `plot_dependence_heatmap` function
trains a random forest for each numeric column from the other
columns in a training dataset. The dependence value is the R2
score from the out-of-bag (OOB) estimates for predicting that
column (see Figure 8-1).

The suggested way to use this plot is to find values close to 1.
The label on the X axis is the feature that predicts the Y axis
label. If a feature predicts another, you can remove the predicted feature (the feature on the Y axis). In our example, `fare`
predicts `pclass`, `sibsp`, `parch`, and `embarked_Q`. We should be
able to keep `fare` and remove the others and get similar
performance:

```
>>> rfpimp.plot_dependence_heatmap(
...     rfpimp.feature_dependence_matrix(X_train),
...     value_fontsize=12,
...     label_fontsize=14,
...     figsize=(8, 8),sn
... )
>>> fig = plt.gcf()
>>> fig.savefig(
...     "images/mlpr_0801.png",
...     dpi=300,
...     bbox_inches="tight",
... )
```

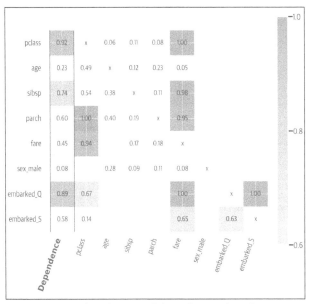

Figure 8-1. Dependence heat map. Pclass, sibsp, parch, and embarked_Q can be predicted from fare, so we can remove them.

Here is code showing that we get a similar score if we remove these columns:

```
>>> cols_to_remove = [
...     "pclass",
...     "sibsp",
...     "parch",
...     "embarked_Q",
... ]
>>> rf3 = RandomForestClassifier(random_state=42)
>>> rf3.fit(
...     X_train[
...         [
...             c
...             for c in X_train.columns
...             if c not in cols_to_remove
...         ]
...     ],
...     y_train,
... )
>>> rf3.score(
...     X_test[
...         [
...             c
...             for c in X_train.columns
...             if c not in cols_to_remove
...         ]
...     ],
...     y_test,
... )
0.7684478371501272

>>> rf4 = RandomForestClassifier(random_state=42)
>>> rf4.fit(X_train, y_train)
>>> rf4.score(X_test, y_test)
0.7659033078880407
```

Lasso Regression

If you use lasso regression, you can set an alpha parameter that
acts as a regularization parameter. As you increase the value, it
gives less weight to features that are less important. Here we use

the LassoLarsCV model to iterate over various values of alpha
and track the feature coefficients (see Figure 8-2):

```
>>> from sklearn import linear_model
>>> model = linear_model.LassoLarsCV(
...     cv=10, max_n_alphas=10
... ).fit(X_train, y_train)
>>> fig, ax = plt.subplots(figsize=(12, 8))
>>> cm = iter(
...     plt.get_cmap("tab20")(
...         np.linspace(0, 1, X.shape[1])
...     )
... )
>>> for i in range(X.shape[1]):
...     c = next(cm)
...     ax.plot(
...         model.alphas_,
...         model.coef_path_.T[:, i],
...         c=c,
...         alpha=0.8,
...         label=X.columns[i],
...     )
>>> ax.axvline(
...     model.alpha_,
...     linestyle="-",
...     c="k",
...     label="alphaCV",
... )
>>> plt.ylabel("Regression Coefficients")
>>> ax.legend(X.columns, bbox_to_anchor=(1, 1))
>>> plt.xlabel("alpha")
>>> plt.title(
...     "Regression Coefficients Progression for
Lasso Paths"
... )
>>> fig.savefig(
...     "images/mlpr_0802.png",
...     dpi=300,
...     bbox_inches="tight",
... )
```

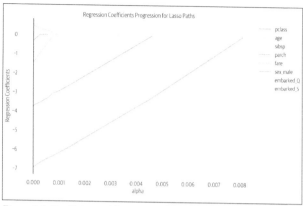

Figure 8-2. Coefficients of features as alpha varies during lasso regression.

Recursive Feature Elimination

Recursive feature elimination will remove the weakest features, then fit a model (see Figure 8-3). It does this by passing in a scikit-learn model with a .coef_ or .feature_importances_ attribute:

```
>>> from yellowbrick.features import RFECV
>>> fig, ax = plt.subplots(figsize=(6, 4))
>>> rfe = RFECV(
...        ensemble.RandomForestClassifier(
...            n_estimators=100
...        ),
...        cv=5,
... )
>>> rfe.fit(X, y)

>>> rfe.rfe_estimator_.ranking_
array([1, 1, 2, 3, 1, 1, 5, 4])

>>> rfe.rfe_estimator_.n_features_
4
```

```
>>> rfe.rfe_estimator_.support_
array([ True,  True, False, False,  True,
        True, False, False])

>>> rfe.poof()
>>> fig.savefig("images/mlpr_0803.png", dpi=300)
```

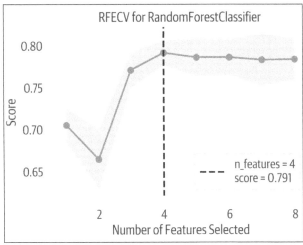

Figure 8-3. Recursive feature elimination.

We will use recursive feature elimination to find the 10 most important features. (In this aggregated dataset we find that we have leaked the survival column!)

```
>>> from sklearn.feature_selection import RFE
>>> model = ensemble.RandomForestClassifier(
...     n_estimators=100
... )
>>> rfe = RFE(model, 4)
>>> rfe.fit(X, y)
>>> agg_X.columns[rfe.support_]
Index(['pclass', 'age', 'fare', 'sex_male'],
dtype='object')
```

Mutual Information

Sklearn provides nonparametric tests that will use k-nearest neighbor to determine the *mutual information* between features and the target. Mutual information quantifies the amount of information gained by observing another variable. The value is zero or more. If the value is zero, then there is no relation between them (see Figure 8-4). This number is not bounded and represents the number of *bits* shared between the feature and the target:

```
>>> from sklearn import feature_selection

>>> mic = feature_selection.mutual_info_classif(
...     X, y
... )
>>> fig, ax = plt.subplots(figsize=(10, 8))
>>> (
...     pd.DataFrame(
...         {"feature": X.columns, "vimp": mic}
...     )
...     .set_index("feature")
...     .plot.barh(ax=ax)
... )
>>> fig.savefig("images/mlpr_0804.png")
```

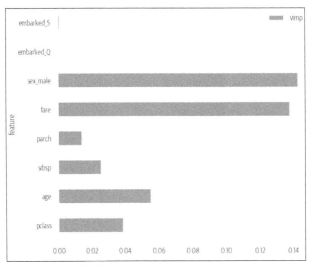

Figure 8-4. Mutual information plot.

Principal Component Analysis

Another option for feature selection is to run principal component analysis. Once you have the main principal components, examine the features that contribute to them the most. These are features that have more variance. Note that this is an unsupervised algorithm and doesn't take y into account.

See "PCA" on page 239 for more details.

Feature Importance

Most tree models provide access to a `.feature_importances_` attribute following training. A higher importance typically means that there is higher error when the feature is removed from the model. See the chapters for the various tree models for more details.

CHAPTER 9

Imbalanced Classes

If you are classifying data, and the classes are not relatively balanced in size, the bias toward more popular classes can carry over into your model. For example, if you have 1 positive case and 99 negative cases, you can get 99% accuracy simply by classifying everything as negative. There are various options for dealing with *imbalanced classes*.

Use a Different Metric

One hint is to use a measure other than accuracy (AUC is a good choice) for calibrating models. Precision and recall are also better options when the target sizes are different. However, there are other options to consider as well.

Tree-based Algorithms and Ensembles

Tree-based models may perform better depending on the distribution of the smaller class. If they tend to be clustered, they can be classified easier.

Ensemble methods can further aid in pulling out the minority classes. Bagging and boosting are options found in tree models like random forests and Extreme Gradient Boosting (XGBoost).

Penalize Models

Many scikit-learn classification models support the `class_weight` parameter. Setting this to `'balanced'` will attempt to regularize minority classes and incentivize the model to classify them correctly. Alternatively, you can grid search and specify the weight options by passing in a dictionary mapping class to weight (give higher weight to smaller classes).

The XGBoost (*https://xgboost.readthedocs.io*) library has the `max_delta_step` parameter, which can be set from 1 to 10 to make the update step more conservative. It also has the `scale_pos_weight` parameter that sets the ratio of negative to positive samples (for binary classes). Also, the `eval_metric` should be set to `'auc'` rather than the default value of `'error'` for classification.

The KNN model has a `weights` parameter that can bias neighbors that are closer. If the minority class samples are close together, setting this parameter to `'distance'` may improve performance.

Upsampling Minority

You can upsample the minority class in a couple of ways. Here is an sklearn implementation:

```
>>> from sklearn.utils import resample
>>> mask = df.survived == 1
>>> surv_df = df[mask]
>>> death_df = df[~mask]
>>> df_upsample = resample(
...     surv_df,
...     replace=True,
...     n_samples=len(death_df),
...     random_state=42,
... )
>>> df2 = pd.concat([death_df, df_upsample])

>>> df2.survived.value_counts()
```

```
1    809
0    809
Name: survived, dtype: int64
```

We can also use the imbalanced-learn library to randomly sample with replacement:

```
>>> from imblearn.over_sampling import (
...     RandomOverSampler,
... )
>>> ros = RandomOverSampler(random_state=42)
>>> X_ros, y_ros = ros.fit_sample(X, y)
>>> pd.Series(y_ros).value_counts()
1    809
0    809
dtype: int64
```

Generate Minority Data

The imbalanced-learn library can also generate new samples of minority classes with both the Synthetic Minority Oversampling Technique (SMOTE) and Adaptive Synthetic (ADASYN) sampling approach algorithms. SMOTE works by choosing one of its k-nearest neighbors, connecting a line to one of them, and choosing a point along that line. ADASYN is similar to SMOTE, but generates more samples from those that are harder to learn. The classes in imbanced-learn are named over_sampling.SMOTE and over_sampling.ADASYN.

Downsampling Majority

Another method to balance classes is to downsample majority classes. Here is an sklearn example:

```
>>> from sklearn.utils import resample
>>> mask = df.survived == 1
>>> surv_df = df[mask]
>>> death_df = df[~mask]
>>> df_downsample = resample(
...     death_df,
...     replace=False,
```

```
...         n_samples=len(surv_df),
...         random_state=42,
... )
>>> df3 = pd.concat([surv_df, df_downsample])

>>> df3.survived.value_counts()
1    500
0    500
Name: survived, dtype: int64
```

TIP

Don't use replacement when downsampling.

The imbalanced-learn library also implements various down-sampling algorithms:

ClusterCentroids
> This class uses K-means to synthesize data with the centroids.

RandomUnderSampler
> This class randomly selects samples.

NearMiss
> This class uses nearest neighbors to downsample.

TomekLink
> This class downsamples by removing samples that are close to each other.

EditedNearestNeighbours
> This class removes samples that have neighbors that are either not in the majority or all of the same class.

RepeatedNearestNeighbours
> This class repeatedly calls the EditedNearestNeighbours.

AllKNN

> This class is similar but increases the number of nearest neighbors during the iterations of downsampling.

CondensedNearestNeighbour

> This class picks one sample of the class to be downsampled, then iterates through the other samples of the class, and if KNN doesn't misclassify, it adds that sample.

OneSidedSelection

> This classremoves noisy samples.

NeighbourhoodCleaningRule

> This class uses EditedNearestNeighbours results and applies KNN to it.

InstanceHardnessThreshold

> This class trains a model, then removes samples with low probabilities.

All of these classes support the .fit_sample method.

Upsampling Then Downsampling

The imbalanced-learn library implements SMOTEENN and SMOTE Tomek, which both upsample and then apply downsampling to clean up the data.

CHAPTER 10

Classification

Classification is a *supervised learning* mechanism for labeling a sample based on the features. Supervised learning means that we have labels for classification or numbers for regression that the algorithm should learn.

We will look at various classification models in this chapter. Sklearn implements many common and useful models. We will also see some that are not in sklearn, but implement the sklearn interface. Because they follow the same interface, it is easy to try different families of models and see how well they perform.

In sklearn, we create a model instance and call the `.fit` method on it with the training data and training labels. We can now call the `.predict` method (or the `.predict_proba` or the `.predict_log_proba` methods) with the fitted model. To evaluate the model, we use the `.score` with testing data and testing labels.

The bigger challenge is usually arranging data in a form that will work with sklearn. The data (X) should be an (m by n) numpy array (or pandas DataFrame) with m rows of sample data each with n features (columns). The label (y) is a vector (or pandas series) of size m with a value (class) for each sample.

The .score method returns the mean accuracy, which by itself might not be sufficient to evaluate a classifier. We will see other evaluation metrics.

We will look at many models and discuss their efficiency, the preprocessing techniques they require, how to prevent overfitting, and if the model supports intuitive interpretation of results.

The general methods that sklearn type models implement are:

`fit(X, y[, sample_weight])`
> Fit a model

`predict(X)`
> Predict classes

`predict_log_proba(X)`
> Predict log probability

`predict_proba(X)`
> Predict probability

`score(X, y[, sample_weight])`
> Get accuracy

Logistic Regression

Logistic regression estimates probabilities by using a logistic function. (Careful; even though it has regression in the name, it is used for classification.) This has been the standard classification model for most sciences.

The following are some model characteristics that we will include for each model:

Runtime efficiency
> Can use `n_jobs` if not using `'liblinear'` solver.

Preprocess data
> If `solver` is set to `'sag'` or `'saga'`, standardize so that convergence works. Can handle sparse input.

Prevent overfitting

The C parameter controls regularization. (Lower C is more regularization, higher means less.) Can specify penalty to 'l1' or 'l2' (the default).

Interpret results

The .coef_ attribute of the fitted model shows the decision function coefficients. A change in x one unit changes the log odds ratio by the coefficient. The .intercept_ attribute is the inverse log odds of the baseline condition.

Here is an example using this model:

```
>>> from sklearn.linear_model import (
...     LogisticRegression,
... )
>>> lr = LogisticRegression(random_state=42)
>>> lr.fit(X_train, y_train)
LogisticRegression(C=1.0, class_weight=None,
    dual=False, fit_intercept=True,
    intercept_scaling=1, max_iter=100,
    multi_class='ovr', n_jobs=1, penalty='l2',
    random_state=42, solver='liblinear',
    tol=0.0001, verbose=0, warm_start=False)
>>> lr.score(X_test, y_test)
0.8040712468193384

>>> lr.predict(X.iloc[[0]])
array([1])
>>> lr.predict_proba(X.iloc[[0]])
array([[0.08698937, 0.91301063]])
>>> lr.predict_log_proba(X.iloc[[0]])
array([[-2.4419694 , -0.09100775]])
>>> lr.decision_function(X.iloc[[0]])
array([2.35096164])
```

Instance parameters:

penalty='l2'
    Penalization norm, 'l1' or 'l2'.

`dual=False`
Use dual formulation (only with `'l2'` and `'liblinear'`).

`C=1.0`
Positive float. Inverse regularization strength. Smaller is stronger regularization.

`fit_intercept=True`
Add bias to the decision function.

`intercept_scaling=1`
If `fit_intercept` and `'liblinear'`, scale the intercept.

`max_iter=100`
Maximum number of iterations.

`multi_class='ovr'`
Use one versus rest for each class, or for `'multinomial'`, train one class.

`class_weight=None`
Dictionary or `'balanced'`.

`solver='liblinear'`
`'liblinear'` is good for small data. `'newton-cg'`, `'sag'`, `'saga'`, and `'lbfgs'` are for multiclass data. `'liblinear'` and `'saga'` only work with `'l1'` penalty. The others work with `'l2'`.

`tol=0.0001`
Stopping tolerance.

`verbose=0`
Be verbose (if nonzero int).

`warm_start=False`
If `True`, remember previous fit.

`njobs=1`
Number of CPUs to use. `-1` is all. Only works with `multi_class='over'` and solver is not `'liblinear'`.

Attributes after fitting:

`coef_`
Decision function coefficients

`intercept_`
Intercept of the decision function

`n_iter_`
Number of iterations

The intercept is the log odds of the baseline condition. We can convert it back to a percent accuracy (proportion):

```
>>> lr.intercept_
array([-0.62386001])
```

Using the inverse logit function, we see that the baseline for survival is 34%:

```
>>> def inv_logit(p):
...     return np.exp(p) / (1 + np.exp(p))

>>> inv_logit(lr.intercept_)
array([0.34890406])
```

We can inspect the coefficients. The inverse logit of the coefficients gives the proportion of the positive cases. In this case, if fare goes up, we are more likely to survive. If sex is male, we are less likely to survive:

```
>>> cols = X.columns
>>> for col, val in sorted(
...     zip(cols, lr.coef_[0]),
...     key=lambda x: x[1],
...     reverse=True,
... ):
...     print(
...         f"{col:10}{val:10.3f} {inv_logit(val):
10.3f}"
...     )
fare          0.104      0.526
parch        -0.062      0.485
```

sibsp	-0.274	0.432
age	-0.296	0.427
embarked_Q	-0.504	0.377
embarked_S	-0.507	0.376
pclass	-0.740	0.323
sex_male	-2.400	0.083

Yellowbrick can also visualize the coefficients. This visualizer has a relative=True parameter that makes the largest value be 100 (or -100), and the others are the percentages of that (see Figure 10-1):

```
>>> from yellowbrick.features.importances import (
...     FeatureImportances,
... )
>>> fig, ax = plt.subplots(figsize=(6, 4))
>>> fi_viz = FeatureImportances(lr)
>>> fi_viz.fit(X, y)
>>> fi_viz.poof()
>>> fig.savefig("images/mlpr_1001.png", dpi=300)
```

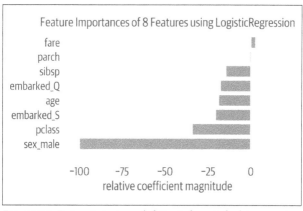

Figure 10-1. Feature importance (relative to largest absolute regression coefficient).

Naive Bayes

Naive Bayes is a probabilistic classifier that assumes independence between the features of the data. It is popular for text classification applications, such as catching spam. One advantage of this model is that because it assumes feature independence, it can train a model with a small number of samples. (A downside is that it can't capture the interactions between features.) This simple model can also work with data that has many features. As such, it serves as a good baseline model.

There are three classes in sklearn: `GaussianNB`, `MultinomialNB`, and `BernoulliNB`. The first assumes a Gaussian distribution (continuous features with a normal distribution), the second is for discrete occurrence counts, and the third is for discrete Boolean features.

This model has the following properties:

Runtime efficiency
> Training O(Nd), where N is the number of training examples and d is dimensionality. Testing O(cd), where c is the number of classes.

Preprocess data
> Assumes that data is independent. Should perform better after removing colinear columns. For continuous numerical data, might be good to bin data. Gaussian assumes normal distribution, and you might need to transform data to convert to normal distribution.

Prevent overfitting
> Exhibits high bias and low variance (ensembles won't reduce variance).

Interpret results
> Percentage is the likelihood that a sample belongs to a class based on priors.

Here is an example using this model:

```
>>> from sklearn.naive_bayes import GaussianNB
>>> nb = GaussianNB()
>>> nb.fit(X_train, y_train)
GaussianNB(priors=None, var_smoothing=1e-09)
>>> nb.score(X_test, y_test)
0.7837150127226463

>>> nb.predict(X.iloc[[0]])
array([1])
>>> nb.predict_proba(X.iloc[[0]])
array([[2.17472227e-08, 9.99999978e-01]])
>>> nb.predict_log_proba(X.iloc[[0]])
array([[-1.76437798e+01, -2.17472227e-08]])
```

Instance parameters:

priors=None
    Prior probabilities of classes.

var_smoothing=1e-9
    Added to variance for stable calculations.

Attributes after fitting:

class_prior_
    Probabilities of classes

class_count_
    Counts of classes

theta_
    Mean of each column per class

sigma_
    Variance of each column per class

epsilon_
    Additive value to each variance

Support Vector Machine

A Support Vector Machine (SVM) is an algorithm that tries to fit a line (or plane or hyperplane) between the different classes that maximizes the distance from the line to the points of the classes. In this way it tries to find a robust separation between the classes. The *support vectors* are the points of the edge of the dividing hyperplane.

SVM generally performs well and can support linear spaces or nonlinear spaces by using a *kernel trick*. The kernel trick is the idea that we can create a decision boundary in a new dimension by minimizing a formula that is easier to calculate than actually mapping the points to the new dimension. The default kernel is the Radial Basis Function (`'rbf'`), which is controlled by the `gamma` parameter and can map an input space into a high dimensional space.

SVMs have the following properties:

Runtime efficiency
> The scikit-learn implementation is $O(n^4)$, so it can be hard to scale to large sizes. Using a linear kernel or the Line arSVC model can improve the runtime performance at perhaps the cost of accuracy. Upping the cache_size parameter can bring that down to $O(n^3)$.

Preprocess data
> The algorithm is not scale invariant. Standardizing the data is highly recommended.

Prevent overfitting
> The C (penalty parameter) controls regularization. A smaller value allows for a smaller margin in the hyperplane. A higher value for gamma will tend to overfit the training data. The LinearSVC model supports a loss and penalty parameter to support regularization.

Interpret results
> Inspect .support_vectors_, though these are hard to explain. With linear kernels, you can inspect .coef_.

Here is an example using scikit-learn's SVM implementation:

```
>>> from sklearn.svm import SVC
>>> svc = SVC(random_state=42, probability=True)
>>> svc.fit(X_train, y_train)
SVC(C=1.0, cache_size=200, class_weight=None,
  coef0=0.0, decision_function_shape='ovr',
  degree=3, gamma='auto', kernel='rbf',
  max_iter=-1, probability=True, random_state=42,
  shrinking=True, tol=0.001, verbose=False)
>>> svc.score(X_test, y_test)
0.8015267175572519

>>> svc.predict(X.iloc[[0]])
array([1])
>>> svc.predict_proba(X.iloc[[0]])
array([[0.15344656, 0.84655344]])
```

```
>>> svc.predict_log_proba(X.iloc[[0]])
array([[-1.87440289, -0.16658195]])
```

To get probability, use `probability=True`, which will slow down fitting of the model.

This is similar to a perceptron, but will find the maximum margin. If the data is not linearly separable, it will minimize the error. Alternatively, a different kernel may be used.

Instance parameters:

`C=1.0`
> The penalty parameter. The smaller the value, the tighter the decision boundary (more overfitting).

`cache_size=200`
> Cache size (MB). Bumping this up can improve training time on large datasets.

`class_weight=None`
> Dictionary or `'balanced'`. Use dictionary to set `C` for each class.

`coef0=0.0`
> Independent term for poly and sigmoid kernels.

`decision_function_shape='ovr'`
> Use one versus rest (`'ovr'`) or one versus one.

`degree=3`
> Degree for polynomial kernel.

`gamma='auto'`
> Kernel coefficient. Can be a number, `'scale'` (default in 0.22, 1 / (num features * X.std())), or `'auto'` (default prior, 1 / num features). A lower value leads to overfitting the training data.

`kernel='rbf'`
> Kernel type: `'linear'`, `'poly'`, `'rbf'` (default), `'sigmoid'`, `'precomputed'`, or a function.

`max_iter=-1`
Maximum number of iterations for solver. -1 for no limit.

`probability=False`
Enable probability estimation. Slows down training.

`random_state=None`
Random seed.

`shrinking=True`
Use shrinking heuristic.

`tol=0.001`
Stopping tolerance.

`verbose=False`
Verbosity.

Attributes after fitting:

`support_`
Support vector indices

`support_vectors_`
Support vectors

`n_support_vectors_`
Count of per-class support vectors

`coef_`
Coefficients (for linear) kernel

K-Nearest Neighbor

The K-Nearest Neighbor (KNN) algorithm classifies based on distance to some number (k) of training samples. The algorithm family is called *instance-based* learning as there are no parameters to learn. This model assumes that distance is sufficient for inference; otherwise it makes no assumptions about the underlying data or its distributions.

The tricky part is selecting the appropriate k value. Also, the curse of dimensionality can hamper distance metrics as there is little difference in high dimensions between nearest and farthest neighbor.

Nearest neighbor models have the following properties:

Runtime efficiency
Training $O(1)$, but need to store data. Testing $O(Nd)$ where N is the number of training examples and d is dimensionality.

Preprocess data
Yes, distance-based calculations perform better when standardized.

Prevent overfitting
Raise n_neighbors. Change p for L1 or L2 metric.

Interpret results
Interpret the k-nearest neighbors to the sample (using the .kneighbors method). Those neighbors (if you can explain them) explain your result.

Here is an example of using the model:

```
>>> from sklearn.neighbors import (
...     KNeighborsClassifier,
... )
>>> knc = KNeighborsClassifier()
>>> knc.fit(X_train, y_train)
KNeighborsClassifier(algorithm='auto',
  leaf_size=30, metric='minkowski',
  metric_params=None, n_jobs=1, n_neighbors=5,
  p=2, weights='uniform')
>>> knc.score(X_test, y_test)
0.7837150127226463

>>> knc.predict(X.iloc[[0]])
array([1])

>>> knc.predict_proba(X.iloc[[0]])
array([[0., 1.]])
```

Attributes:

`algorithm='auto'`
    Can be `'brute'`, `'ball_tree'`, or `'kd_tree'`.

`leaf_size=30`
    Used for tree algorithms.

`metric='minkowski'`
    Distance metric.

`metric_params=None`
    Additional dictionary of parameters for custom metric function.

`n_jobs=1`
    Number of CPUs.

`n_neighbors=5`
    Number of neighbors.

`p=2`
    Minkowski power parameter: 1 = manhattan (L1). 2 = Euclidean (L2).

`weights='uniform'`
    Can be `'distance'`, in which case, closer points have more influence.

Distance metrics include: `'euclidean'`, `'manhattan'`, `'chebyshev'`, `'minkowski'`, `'wminkowski'`, `'seuclidean'`, `'mahalanobis'`, `'haversine'`, `'hamming'`, `'canberra'`, `'braycurtis'`, `'jaccard'`, `'matching'`, `'dice'`, `'rogerstanimoto'`, `'russellrao'`, `'sokalmichener'`, `'sokalsneath'`, or a callable (user defined).

NOTE

If k is an even number and the neighbors are split, the result depends on the order of the training data.

Decision Tree

A decision tree is like going to a doctor who asks a series of questions to determine the cause of your symptoms. We can use a process to create a decision tree and have a series of questions to predict a target class. The advantages of this model include support for nonnumeric data (in some implementations), little data preparation (no need for scaling), support for dealing with nonlinear relationships, feature importances are revealed, and it is easy to explain.

The default algorithm used for creation is called the classification and regression tree (CART). It uses the Gini impurity or index measure to construct decisions. This is done by looping over the features and finding the value that gives the lowest probability of misclassifying.

TIP

The default values will lead to a fully grown (read overfit) tree. Use a mechanism such as max_depth and cross-validation to control for this.

Decision trees have the following properties:

Runtime efficiency
For creation, loop over each of the m features, and sort all n samples, O(mn log n). For predicting, you walk the tree, O(height).

Preprocess data
Scaling is not necessary. Need to get rid of missing values and convert to numeric.

Prevent overfitting
Set max_depth to a lower number, raise min_impurity_decrease.

Interpret results

> Can step through the tree of choices. Because there are steps, a tree is bad at dealing with linear relationships (a small change in a number can go down a different path). The tree is also highly dependent on the training data. A small change can change the whole tree.

Here is an example using the scikit-learn library:

```
>>> from sklearn.tree import DecisionTreeClassifier
>>> dt = DecisionTreeClassifier(
...     random_state=42, max_depth=3
... )
>>> dt.fit(X_train, y_train)
DecisionTreeClassifier(class_weight=None,
  criterion='gini', max_depth=None,
  max_features=None, max_leaf_nodes=None,
  min_impurity_decrease=0.0,
  min_impurity_split=None,
  min_samples_leaf=1, min_samples_split=2,
  min_weight_fraction_leaf=0.0, presort=False,
  random_state=42, splitter='best')

>>> dt.score(X_test, y_test)
0.8142493638676844

>>> dt.predict(X.iloc[[0]])
array([1])
>>> dt.predict_proba(X.iloc[[0]])
array([[0.02040816, 0.97959184]])
>>> dt.predict_log_proba(X.iloc[[0]])
array([[-3.8918203 , -0.02061929]])
```

Instance parameters:

class_weight=None

> Weights for class in dictionary. 'balanced' will set values to the inverse proportion of class frequencies. Default is a value of 1 for each class. For multiclass, need a list of dictionaries, one-versus-rest (OVR) for each class.

```
criterion='gini'
```
Splitting function, `'gini'` or `'entropy'`.

```
max_depth=None
```
Depth of tree. Default will build until the leaves contain less than `min_samples_split`.

```
max_features=None
```
Number of features to examine for split. Default is all.

```
max_leaf_nodes=None
```
Limit the number of leaves. Default is unlimited.

```
min_impurity_decrease=0.0
```
Split node if a split will decrease impurity >= value.

```
min_impurity_split=None
```
Deprecated.

```
min_samples_leaf=1
```
Minimum number of samples at each leaf.

```
min_samples_split=2
```
Minimum number of samples required to split a node.

```
min_weight_fraction_leaf=0.0
```
Minimum sum total of weights required for leaf nodes.

```
presort=False
```
May speed up training with a small dataset or restricted depth if set to `True`.

```
random_state=None
```
Random seed.

```
splitter='best'
```
Use `'random'` or `'best'`.

Attributes after fitting:

```
classes_
```
Class labels

```
feature_importances_
```
Array of Gini importance

n_classes_
    Number of classes

n_features_
    Number of features

tree_
    Underlying tree object

View the tree with this code (see Figure 10-2):

```
>>> import pydotplus
>>> from io import StringIO
>>> from sklearn.tree import export_graphviz
>>> dot_data = StringIO()
>>> tree.export_graphviz(
...     dt,
...     out_file=dot_data,
...     feature_names=X.columns,
...     class_names=["Died", "Survived"],
...     filled=True,
... )
>>> g = pydotplus.graph_from_dot_data(
...     dot_data.getvalue()
... )
>>> g.write_png("images/mlpr_1002.png")
```

For Jupyter, use:

```
from IPython.display import Image
Image(g.create_png())
```

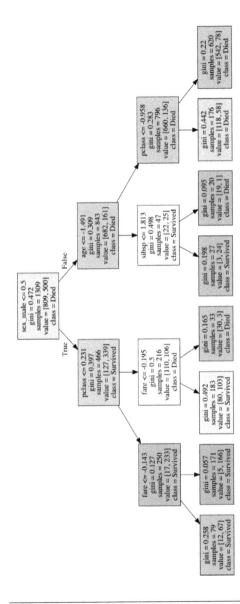

Figure 10-2. Decision tree.

The dtreeviz package (*https://github.com/parrt/dtreeviz*) can aid in understanding how the decision tree works. It creates a tree with labeled histograms, which gives valuable insight (see Figure 10-3). Here is an example. In Jupyter we can just display the viz object directly. If we are working from a script, we can call the .save method to create a PDF, SVG, or PNG:

```
>>> viz = dtreeviz.trees.dtreeviz(
...     dt,
...     X,
...     y,
...     target_name="survived",
...     feature_names=X.columns,
...     class_names=["died", "survived"],
... )
>>> viz
```

Figure 10-3. dtreeviz output.

Feature importance showing Gini importance (reduction of error by using that feature):

```
>>> for col, val in sorted(
...     zip(X.columns, dt.feature_importances_),
...     key=lambda x: x[1],
...     reverse=True,
... )[:5]:
...     print(f"{col:10}{val:10.3f}")
sex_male      0.607
pclass        0.248
sibsp         0.052
fare          0.050
age           0.043
```

You can also use Yellowbrick to visualize feature importance (see Figure 10-4):

```
>>> from yellowbrick.features.importances import (
...     FeatureImportances,
... )
>>> fig, ax = plt.subplots(figsize=(6, 4))
>>> fi_viz = FeatureImportances(dt)
>>> fi_viz.fit(X, y)
>>> fi_viz.poof()
>>> fig.savefig("images/mlpr_1004.png", dpi=300)
```

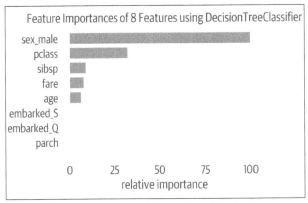

Figure 10-4. Feature importance (Gini coefficient) for decision tree (normalized to male importance).

Random Forest

A random forest is an ensemble of decision trees. It uses *bagging* to correct the tendency of decision trees to overfit. By creating many trees trained on random subsamples of the samples and random features of the data, the variance is lowered.

Because they train on subsamples of the data, random forests can evaluate OOB error and evaluate performance. They can also track feature importance by averaging the feature importance over all of the trees.

The intuition for understanding bagging comes from a 1785 essay by Marquis de Condorcet. The essence is that if you are creating a jury, you should add anyone who has a greater than 50% chance of delivering the correct verdict and then average their decisions. Every time you add another member (and their selection process is independent of the others), you will get a better result.

The idea with random forests is to create a "forest" of decision trees trained on different columns of the training data. If each tree has a better than 50% chance of correct classification, you should incorporate its prediction. The random forest has been an excellent tool for both classification and regression, though it has recently fallen out of favor for gradient-boosted trees.

It has the following properties:

Runtime efficiency
    Need to create j random trees. This can be done in parallel using n_jobs. Complexity for each tree is O(mn log n), where n is the number of samples and m is the number of features. For creation, loop over each of the m features, and sort all n samples, O(mn log n). For predicting, walk the tree O(height).

Preprocess data
    Not necessary.

Prevent overfitting
    Add more trees (n_estimators). Use lower max_depth.

Interpret results
    Supports feature importance, but we don't have a single decision tree that we can walk through. Can inspect single trees from the ensemble.

Here is an example:

```
>>> from sklearn.ensemble import (
...     RandomForestClassifier,
... )
>>> rf = RandomForestClassifier(random_state=42)
>>> rf.fit(X_train, y_train)
RandomForestClassifier(bootstrap=True,
  class_weight=None, criterion='gini',
  max_depth=None, max_features='auto',
  max_leaf_nodes=None, min_impurity_decrease=0.0,
  min_impurity_split=None, min_samples_leaf=1,
  min_samples_split=2,
  min_weight_fraction_leaf=0.0,
  n_estimators=10, n_jobs=1, oob_score=False,
  random_state=42, verbose=0, warm_start=False)
>>> rf.score(X_test, y_test)
```

```
0.7862595419847328

>>> rf.predict(X.iloc[[0]])
array([1])
>>> rf.predict_proba(X.iloc[[0]])
array([[0., 1.]])
>>> rf.predict_log_proba(X.iloc[[0]])
array([[-inf,   0.]])
```

Instance parameters (these options mirror the decision tree):

bootstrap=True
> Bootstrap when building trees.

class_weight=None
> Weights for class in dictionary. 'balanced' will set values
> to the inverse proportion of class frequencies. Default is a
> value of 1 for each class. For multiclass, need a list of dic-
> tionaries (OVR) for each class.

criterion='gini'
> Splitting function, 'gini' or 'entropy'.

max_depth=None
> Depth of tree. Default will build until leaves contain less
> than min_samples_split.

max_features='auto'
> Number of features to examine for split. Default is all.

max_leaf_nodes=None
> Limit the number of leaves. Default is unlimited.

min_impurity_decrease=0.0
> Split node if a split will decrease impurity >= value.

min_impurity_split=None
> Deprecated.

min_samples_leaf=1
> Minimum number of samples at each leaf.

```
min_samples_split=2
```
Minimum number of samples required to split a node. `min_weight_fraction_leaf=0.0`- Minimum sum total of weights required for leaf nodes.

```
*n_estimators=10
```
Number of trees in the forest.

```
n_jobs=1
```
Number of jobs for fitting and predicting.

```
oob_score=False
```
Whether to estimate `oob_score`.

```
random_state=None
```
Random seed.

```
verbose=0
```
Verbosity.

```
warm_start=False
```
Fit a new forest or use the existing one.

Attributes after fitting:

```
classes_
```
Class labels.

```
feature_importances_
```
Array of Gini importance.

```
n_classes_
```
Number of classes.

```
n_features_
```
Number of features.

```
oob_score_
```
OOB score. Average accuracy for each observation not used in trees.

Feature importance showing Gini importance (reduction of error by using that feature):

```
>>> for col, val in sorted(
...     zip(X.columns, rf.feature_importances_),
...     key=lambda x: x[1],
...     reverse=True,
... )[:5]:
...     print(f"{col:10}{val:10.3f}")
age            0.285
fare           0.268
sex_male       0.232
pclass         0.077
sibsp          0.059
```

The random forest classifier computes the feature importance by determining the *mean decrease in impurity* for each feature (also known as Gini importance). Features that reduce uncertainty in classification receive higher scores.

These numbers might be off if features vary in scale or cardinality of categorical columns. A more reliable score is *permutation importance* (where each column has its values permuted and the drop in accuracy is measured). An even more reliable mechanism is *drop column importance* (where each column is dropped and the model is re-evaluated), but sadly this requires creating a new model for each column that is dropped. See the `importances` function in the `rfpimp` package:

```
>>> import rfpimp
>>> rf = RandomForestClassifier(ran
dom_state=42)
>>> rf.fit(X_train, y_train)
>>> rfpimp.importances(
...     rf, X_test, y_test
... ).Importance
Feature
sex_male      0.155216
fare          0.043257
age           0.033079
pclass        0.027990
parch         0.020356
embarked_Q    0.005089
sibsp         0.002545
embarked_S    0.000000
Name: Importance, dtype: float64
```

XGBoost

Although sklearn has a `GradientBoostedClassifier`, it is better to use a third-party implementation that uses extreme boosting. These tend to provide better results.

XGBoost (*https://oreil.ly/WBo0g*) is a popular library outside of scikit-learn. It creates a weak tree and then "boosts" the subsequent trees to reduce the residual errors. It tries to capture and address any patterns in the errors until they appear to be random.

XGBoost has the following properties:

Runtime efficiency
> XGBoost is parallelizeable. Use the `n_jobs` option to indicate the number of CPUs. Use GPU for even better performance.

Preprocess data
> No scaling necessary with tree models. Need to encode categorical data.

Prevent overfitting
> The `early_stopping_rounds=N` parameter can be set to stop training if there is no improvement after N rounds. L1 and L2 regularization are controlled by `reg_alpha` and `reg_lambda`, respectively. Higher numbers are more conservative.

Interpret results
> Has feature importance.

XGBoost has an extra parameter for the `.fit` method. The `early_stopping_rounds` parameter can be combined with the `eval_set` parameter to tell XGBoost to stop creating trees if the evaluation metric has not improved after that many boosting rounds. The `eval_metric` can also be set to one of the following: `'rmse'`, `'mae'`, `'logloss'`, `'error'` (default), `'auc'`, `'aucpr'`, as well as a custom function.

Here is an example using the library:

```
>>> import xgboost as xgb
>>> xgb_class = xgb.XGBClassifier(random_state=42)
>>> xgb_class.fit(
...     X_train,
...     y_train,
...     early_stopping_rounds=10,
...     eval_set=[(X_test, y_test)],
... )
XGBClassifier(base_score=0.5, booster='gbtree',
  colsample_bylevel=1, colsample_bytree=1, gamma=0,
  learning_rate=0.1, max_delta_step=0, max_depth=3,
  min_child_weight=1, missing=None,
  n_estimators=100, n_jobs=1, nthread=None,
  objective='binary:logistic', random_state=42,
  reg_alpha=0, reg_lambda=1, scale_pos_weight=1,
  seed=None, silent=True, subsample=1)

>>> xgb_class.score(X_test, y_test)
0.7862595419847328

>>> xgb_class.predict(X.iloc[[0]])
array([1])
>>> xgb_class.predict_proba(X.iloc[[0]])
array([[0.06732017, 0.93267983]], dtype=float32)
```

Instance parameters:

max_depth=3
    Maximum depth.

learning_rate=0.1
    Learning rate (also called eta) for boosting (between 0 and
    1). After each boost step, the newly added weights are
    scaled by this factor. The lower the value, the more conser-
    vative, but will also need more trees to converge. In the
    call to .train, you can pass a learning_rates parameter,
    which is a list of rates at each round (i.e., [.1]*100 + [.
    05]*100).

```
n_estimators=100
```
Number of rounds or boosted trees.

```
silent=True
```
Opposite of verbose. Whether to print messages while running boosting.

```
objective='binary:logistic'
```
Learning task or callable for classification.

```
booster='gbtree'
```
Can be 'gbtree', 'gblinear', or 'dart'.

```
nthread=None
```
Deprecated.

```
n_jobs=1
```
Number of threads to use.

```
gamma=0
```
Controls pruning. Range is 0 to infinite. Minimum loss reduction needed to further split a leaf. Higher gamma is more conservative. If training and test scores are diverging, insert a higher number (around 10). If training and test scores are close, use a lower number.

```
min_child_weight=1
```
Minimum value for sum of hessian for a child.

```
max_delta_step=0
```
Make update more conservative. Set 1 to 10 for imbalanced classes.

```
subsample=1
```
Fraction of samples to use for next round.

```
colsample_bytree=1
```
Fraction of columns to use for round.

```
colsample_bylevel=1
```
Fraction of columns to use for level.

```
colsample_bynode=1
```
Fraction of columns to use for node.

`reg_alpha=0`

L1 regularization (mean of weights) encourages sparsity. Increase to be more conservative.

`reg_lambda=1`

L2 regularization (root of squared weights) encourages small weights. Increase to be more conservative.

`scale_pos_weight=1`

Ratio of negative/positive weight.

`base_score=.5`

Initial prediction.

`seed=None`

Deprecated.

`random_state=0`

Random seed.

`missing=None`

Value to interpret for `missing`. `None` means `np.nan`.

`importance_type='gain'`

The feature importance type: `'gain'`, `'weight'`, `'cover'`, `'total_gain'`, or `'total_cover'`.

Attributes:

`coef_`

Coefficients for gblinear learners

`feature_importances_`

Feature importances for gbtree learners

Feature importance is the average gain across all the nodes where the feature is used:

```
>>> for col, val in sorted(
...     zip(
...         X.columns,
...         xgb_class.feature_importances_,
...     ),
...     key=lambda x: x[1],
```

```
...       reverse=True,
... )[:5]:
...       print(f"{col:10}{val:10.3f}")
fare           0.420
age            0.309
pclass         0.071
sex_male       0.066
sibsp          0.050
```

XGBoost can plot the feature importance (see Figure 10-5). It has an `importance_type` parameter. The default value is `"weight"`, which is the number of times a feature appears in a tree. It can also be `"gain"`, which shows the average gain when the feature is used, or `"cover"`, which is the number of samples affected by a split:

```
>>> fig, ax = plt.subplots(figsize=(6, 4))
>>> xgb.plot_importance(xgb_class, ax=ax)
>>> fig.savefig("images/mlpr_1005.png", dpi=300)
```

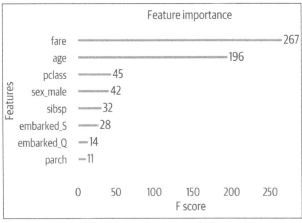

Figure 10-5. Feature importance showing weight (how many times a feature appears in the trees).

We can plot this in Yellowbrick, which normalizes the values (see Figure 10-6):

```
>>> fig, ax = plt.subplots(figsize=(6, 4))
>>> fi_viz = FeatureImportances(xgb_class)
>>> fi_viz.fit(X, y)
>>> fi_viz.poof()
>>> fig.savefig("images/mlpr_1006.png", dpi=300)
```

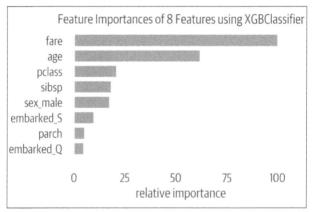

Figure 10-6. Yellowbrick feature importance for XGBoost (normalized to 100).

XGBoost provides both a textual representation of the trees and a graphical one. Here is the text representation:

```
>>> booster = xgb_class.get_booster()
>>> print(booster.get_dump()[0])
0:[sex_male<0.5] yes=1,no=2,missing=1
  1:[pclass<0.23096] yes=3,no=4,missing=3
    3:[fare<-0.142866] yes=7,no=8,missing=7
      7:leaf=0.132530
      8:leaf=0.184
    4:[fare<-0.19542] yes=9,no=10,missing=9
      9:leaf=0.024598
      10:leaf=-0.1459
  2:[age<-1.4911] yes=5,no=6,missing=5
    5:[sibsp<1.81278] yes=11,no=12,missing=11
```

```
      11:leaf=0.13548
      12:leaf=-0.15000
   6:[pclass<-0.95759] yes=13,no=14,missing=13
      13:leaf=-0.06666
      14:leaf=-0.1487
```

The value in the leaf is the score for class 1. It can be converted into a probability using the logistic function. If the decisions fell through to leaf 7, the probability of class 1 is 53%. This is the score from a single tree. If our model had 100 trees, you would sum up each leaf value and get the probability with the logistic function:

```
>>> # score from first tree leaf 7
>>> 1 / (1 + np.exp(-1 * 0.1238))
0.5309105310475829
```

Here is the graphical version of the first tree in the model (see Figure 10-7):

```
>>> fig, ax = plt.subplots(figsize=(6, 4))
>>> xgb.plot_tree(xgb_class, ax=ax, num_trees=0)
>>> fig.savefig("images/mlpr_1007.png", dpi=300)
```

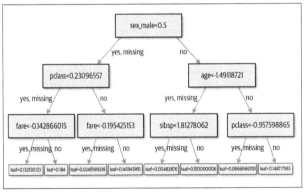

Figure 10-7. Tree of XGBoost.

The xgbfir package (*https://oreil.ly/kPnRv*) is a library built on top of XGBoost. This library gives various measures about feature importance. What is unique is that it provides these measures about the columns, and also pairs of columns, so you can see the interactions. In addition, you can get information about triplets (three-column) interactions.

The measures it provides are:

Gain
Total gain of each feature or feature interaction

FScore
Amount of possible splits taken on a feature or feature interaction

wFScore
Amount of possible splits taken on a feature or feature interaction, weighted by the probability of the splits to take place

Average wFScore
wFScore divided by FScore

Average Gain
Gain divided by FScore

Expected Gain
Total gain of each feature or feature interaction weighted by the probability to gather the gain

The interface is simply an export to a spreadsheet, so we will use pandas to read them back in. Here is the column importance:

```
>>> import xgbfir
>>> xgbfir.saveXgbFI(
...     xgb_class,
...     feature_names=X.columns,
...     OutputXlsxFile="fir.xlsx",
... )
>>> pd.read_excel("/tmp/surv-fir.xlsx").head(3).T
                      0         1         2
Interaction    sex_male    pclass      fare
Gain            1311.44   585.794   544.884
```

FScore	42	45	267
wFScore	39.2892	21.5038	128.33
Average wFScore	0.935458	0.477861	0.480636
Average Gain	31.2247	13.0177	2.04076
Expected Gain	1307.43	229.565	236.738
Gain Rank	1	2	3
FScore Rank	4	3	1
wFScore Rank	3	4	1
Avg wFScore Rank	1	5	4
Avg Gain Rank	1	2	4
Expected Gain Rank	1	3	2
Average Rank	1.83333	3.16667	2.5
Average Tree Index	32.2381	20.9778	51.9101
Average Tree Depth	0.142857	1.13333	1.50562

From this table, we see sex_male ranks high in gain, average wFScore, average gain, and expected gain, whereas fare tops out in FScore and wFScore.

Let's look at pairs of column interactions:

```
>>> pd.read_excel(
...     "fir.xlsx",
...     sheet_name="Interaction Depth 1",
... ).head(2).T
```

Interaction	pclass|sex_male	age|sex_male
Gain	2090.27	964.046
FScore	35	18
wFScore	14.3608	9.65915
Average wFScore	0.410308	0.536619
Average Gain	59.722	53.5581
Expected Gain	827.49	616.17
Gain Rank	1	2
FScore Rank	5	10
wFScore Rank	4	8
Avg wFScore Rank	8	5
Avg Gain Rank	1	2
Expected Gain Rank	1	2
Average Rank	3.33333	4.83333
Average Tree Index	18.9714	38.1111
Average Tree Depth	1	1.11111

Here we see that the top two interactions involve the sex_male column in combination with pclass and age. If you were only able to make a model with two features, you would probably want to choose pclass and sex_male.

Finally, let's look at triplets:

```
>>> pd.read_excel(
...     "fir.xlsx",
...     sheet_name="Interaction Depth 2",
... ).head(1).T
                                    0
Interaction          fare|pclass|sex_male
Gain                            2973.16
FScore                               44
wFScore                         8.92572
Average wFScore                0.202857
Average Gain                    67.5719
Expected Gain                   549.145
Gain Rank                             1
FScore Rank                           1
wFScore Rank                          4
Avg wFScore Rank                     21
Avg Gain Rank                         3
Expected Gain Rank                    2
Average Rank                    5.33333
Average Tree Index              16.6591
Average Tree Depth                    2
```

This is only showing the first triplet due to space limitations, but the spreadsheet has many more:

```
>>> pd.read_excel(
...     "/tmp/surv-fir.xlsx",
...     sheet_name="Interaction Depth 2",
... )[["Interaction", "Gain"]].head()
            Interaction         Gain
0    fare|pclass|sex_male  2973.162529
1     age|pclass|sex_male  1621.945151
2      age|sex_male|sibsp  1042.320428
3      age|fare|sex_male   366.860828
4     fare|fare|sex_male   196.224791
```

Gradient Boosted with LightGBM

LightGBM is an implementation by Microsoft. LightGBM uses a sampling mechanism to deal with continuous values. This allows quicker creation of trees (than say XGBoost), and reduces memory usage.

LightGBM also grows trees depth first (*leaf-wise* rather than *level-wise*). Because of this, rather than using max_depth to control overfitting, use num_leaves (where this value is $< 2^{(max\_depth)}$).

NOTE

Installation of this library currently requires having a compiler and is a little more involved than just a pip install.

It has the following properties:

Runtime efficiency
> Can take advantage of multiple CPUs. By using binning, can be 15 times faster than XGBoost.

Preprocess data
> Has some support for encoding categorical columns as integers (or pandas Categorical type), but AUC appears to suffer compared to one-hot encoding.

Prevent overfitting
> Lower num_leaves. Increase min_data_in_leaf. Use min_gain_to_split with lambda_l1 or lambda_l2.

Interpret results
> Feature importance is available. Individual trees are weak and tend to be hard to interpret.

Here is an example using the library:

```
>>> import lightgbm as lgb
>>> lgbm_class = lgb.LGBMClassifier(
```

```
...        random_state=42
... )
>>> lgbm_class.fit(X_train, y_train)
LGBMClassifier(boosting_type='gbdt',
  class_weight=None, colsample_bytree=1.0,
  learning_rate=0.1, max_depth=-1,
  min_child_samples=20, min_child_weight=0.001,
  min_split_gain=0.0, n_estimators=100,
  n_jobs=-1, num_leaves=31, objective=None,
  random_state=42, reg_alpha=0.0, reg_lambda=0.0,
  silent=True, subsample=1.0,
  subsample_for_bin=200000, subsample_freq=0)

>>> lgbm_class.score(X_test, y_test)
0.7964376590330788

>>> lgbm_class.predict(X.iloc[[0]])
array([1])
>>> lgbm_class.predict_proba(X.iloc[[0]])
array([[0.01637168, 0.98362832]])
```

Instance parameters:

`boosting_type='gbdt'`

Can be: `'gbdt'` (gradient boosting), `'rf'` (random forest), `'dart'` (dropouts meet multiple additive regression trees), or `'goss'` (gradient-based, one-sided sampling).

`class_weight=None`

Dictionary or `'balanced'`. Use dictionary to set weight for each class label when doing multiclass problems. For binary problems, use `is_unbalance` or `scale_pos_weight`.

`colsample_bytree=1.0`

Range (0, 1.0]. Select percent of features for each boosting round.

`importance_type='split'`

How to calculate feature importance. `'split'` means number of times a feature is used. `'gain'` is total gains of splits for a feature.

`learning_rate=0.1`

> Range (0, 1.0]. Learning rate for boosting. A smaller value slows down overfitting as boosting rounds have less impact. A smaller number should give better performance but will require more `num_iterations`.

`max_depth=-1`

> Maximum tree depth. -1 is unlimited. Larger depths tend to overfit more.

`min_child_samples=20`

> Number of samples required for a leaf. Lower numbers mean more overfitting.

`min_child_weight=0.001`

> Sum of hessian weight required for a leaf.

`min_split_gain=0.0`

> Loss reduction required to partition leaf.

`n_estimators=100`

> Number of trees or boosting rounds.

`n_jobs=-1`

> Number of threads.

`num_leaves=31`

> Maximum tree leaves.

`objective=None`

> `None` is `'binary'` or `'multiclass'` for classifier. Can be a function or string.

`random_state=42`

> Random seed.

`reg_alpha=0.0`

> L1 regularization (mean of weights). Increase to be more conservative.

`reg_lambda=0.0`

> L2 regularization (root of squared weights). Increase to be more conservative.

```
silent=True
```
Verbose mode.

```
subsample=1.0
```
Fraction of samples to use for next round.

```
subsample_for_bin=200000
```
Samples required to create bins.

```
subsample_freq=0
```
Subsample frequency. Change to 1 to enable.

Feature importance based on 'splits' (number of times a product is used):

```
>>> for col, val in sorted(
...     zip(cols, lgbm_class.feature_importances_),
...     key=lambda x: x[1],
...     reverse=True,
... )[:5]:
...     print(f"{col:10}{val:10.3f}")
fare        1272.000
age         1182.000
sibsp        118.000
pclass       115.000
sex_male     110.000
```

The LightGBM library supports creating a feature importance plot (see Figure 10-8). The default is based on 'splits', the number of times a feature is used. You can specify 'importance_type' if you want to change it to 'gain':

```
>>> fig, ax = plt.subplots(figsize=(6, 4))
>>> lgb.plot_importance(lgbm_class, ax=ax)
>>> fig.tight_layout()
>>> fig.savefig("images/mlpr_1008.png", dpi=300)
```

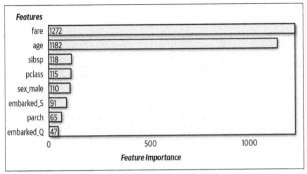

Figure 10-8. Feature importance splits for LightGBM.

WARNING

As of version 0.9, Yellowbrick doesn't work with LightGBM for creating feature importance plots.

We can create a tree of the decisions as well (see Figure 10-9):

```
>>> fig, ax = plt.subplots(figsize=(6, 4))
>>> lgb.plot_tree(lgbm_class, tree_index=0, ax=ax)
>>> fig.savefig("images/mlpr_1009.png", dpi=300)
```

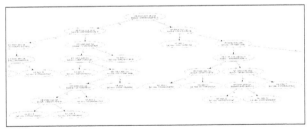

Figure 10-9. LightGBM tree.

TIP

In Jupyter, use the following command to view a tree:

```
lgb.create_tree_digraph(lgbm_class)
```

TPOT

TPOT (*https://oreil.ly/NFJvl*) uses a genetic algorithm to try different models and ensembles. This can take hours to days to run as it considers multiple models and preprocessing steps, as well as the hyperparameters for said models, and ensembling options. On a typical machine, a generation may take five or more minutes to run.

It has the following properties:

Runtime efficiency
    Can take hours or days. Use n_jobs=-1 to use all CPUs.

Preprocess data
    You need to remove NaN and categorical data.

Prevent overfitting
    Ideally, results should use cross-validation to minimize overfitting.

Interpret results
    Depends on the results.

Here is an example of using the library:

```
>>> from tpot import TPOTClassifier
>>> tc = TPOTClassifier(generations=2)
>>> tc.fit(X_train, y_train)
>>> tc.score(X_test, y_test)
0.7888040712468194

>>> tc.predict(X.iloc[[0]])
array([1])
>>> tc.predict_proba(X.iloc[[0]])
array([[0.07449919, 0.92550081]])
```

Instance parameters:

`generations=100`
> Iterations to run.

`population_size=100`
> Population size for genetic programming. Larger size usually performs better but takes more memory and time.

`offspring_size=None`
> Offspring for each generation. Default is `population_size`.

`mutation_rate=.9`
> Mutation rate for algorithm [0, 1]. Default is .9.

`crossover_rate=.1`
> Cross-over rate (how many pipelines to breed in a generation). Range [0, 1]. Default is .1.

`scoring='accuracy'`
> Scoring mechanism. Uses sklearn strings.

`cv=5`
> Cross-validation folds.

`subsample=1`
> Subsample training instances. Range [0, 1]. Default is 1.

`n_jobs=1`
> Number of CPUs to use, -1 for all cores.

`max_time_mins=None`
> Maximum amount of minutes to run.

`max_eval_time_mins=5`
> Maximum amount of minutes to evaluate a single pipeline.

`random_state=None`
> Random seed.

`config_dict`
> Configuration options for optimization.

```
warm_start=False
```
Reuse previous calls to `.fit`.

```
memory=None
```
Can cache pipelines. `'auto'` or a path will persist in a directory.

```
use_dask=False
```
Use dask.

```
periodic_checkpoint_folder=None
```
Path to a folder where the best pipeline will be persisted periodically.

```
early_stop=None
```
Stop after running this many generations with no improvement.

```
verbosity=0
```
0 = none, 1 = minimal, 2 = high, or 3 = all. 2 and higher shows a progress bar.

```
disable_update_check=False
```
Disable version check.

Attributes:

```
evaluated_individuals_
```
Dictionary with all pipelines that were evaluated.

```
fitted_pipeline_
```
Best pipeline.

After you are done, you can export the pipeline:

```
>>> tc.export("tpot_exported_pipeline.py")
```

The result might look like this:

```
import numpy as np
import pandas as pd
from sklearn.ensemble import ExtraTreesClassifier
from sklearn.model_selection import \
    train_test_split
from sklearn.pipeline import make_pipeline, \
```

```
      make_union
from sklearn.preprocessing import Normalizer
from tpot.builtins import StackingEstimator

# NOTE: Make sure that the class is labeled
# 'target' in the data file
tpot_data = pd.read_csv('PATH/TO/DATA/FILE',
    sep='COLUMN_SEPARATOR', dtype=np.float64)
features = tpot_data.drop('target', axis=1).values
training_features, testing_features, \
    training_target, testing_target = \
    train_test_split(features,
        tpot_data['target'].values, random_state=42)

# Score on the training set was:0.8122535043953432
exported_pipeline = make_pipeline(
  Normalizer(norm="max"),
  StackingEstimator(
    estimator=ExtraTreesClassifier(bootstrap=True,
      criterion="gini", max_features=0.85,
      min_samples_leaf=2, min_samples_split=19,
      n_estimators=100)),
  ExtraTreesClassifier(bootstrap=False,
    criterion="entropy", max_features=0.3,
    min_samples_leaf=13, min_samples_split=9,
    n_estimators=100)
)

exported_pipeline.fit(training_features,
  training_target)
results = exported_pipeline.predict(
  testing_features)
```

CHAPTER 11

Model Selection

This chapter will discuss optimizing hyperparameters. It will also explore the issue of whether the model requires more data to perform better.

Validation Curve

Creating a validation curve is one way to determine an appropriate value for a hyperparameter. A validation curve is a plot that shows how the model performance responds to changes in the hyperparameter's value (see Figure 11-1). The chart shows both the training data and the validation data. The validation scores allow us to infer how the model would respond to unseen data. Typically, we would choose a hyperparameter that maximizes the validation score.

In the following example, we will use Yellowbrick to see if changing the value of the `max_depth` hyperparameter changes the model performance of a random forest. You can provide a `scoring` parameter set to a scikit-learn model metric (the default for classification is `'accuracy'`):

```
>>> from yellowbrick.model_selection import (
...     ValidationCurve,
... )
>>> fig, ax = plt.subplots(figsize=(6, 4))
>>> vc_viz = ValidationCurve(
...     RandomForestClassifier(n_estimators=100),
...     param_name="max_depth",
...     param_range=np.arange(1, 11),
...     cv=10,
...     n_jobs=-1,
... )
>>> vc_viz.fit(X, y)
>>> vc_viz.poof()
>>> fig.savefig("images/mlpr_1101.png", dpi=300)
```

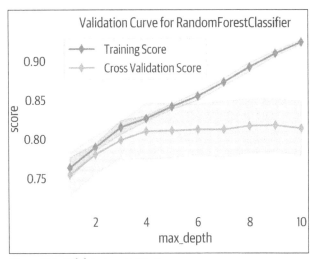

Figure 11-1. Validation curve report.

The ValidationCurve class supports a scoring parameter. The parameter can be a custom function or one of the following options, depending on the task.

Classification scoring options include: 'accuracy', 'aver age_precision', 'f1', 'f1_micro', 'f1_macro', 'f1_weighted', 'f1_samples', 'neg_log_loss', 'precision', 'recall', and 'roc_auc'.

Clustering scoring options: 'adjusted_mutual_info_score', 'adjusted_rand_score', 'completeness_score', 'fowlkesmallows_score', 'homogeneity_score', 'mutual_info_score', 'normalized_mutual_info_score', and 'v_measure_score'.

Regression scoring options: 'explained_variance', 'neg_mean_absolute_error', 'neg_mean_squared_error', 'neg_mean_squared_log_error', 'neg_median_absolute_error', and 'r2'.

Learning Curve

To select the best model for your project, how much data do you need? A learning curve can help us answer that question. This curve plots the training and cross-validation score as we create models with more samples. If the cross-validation score continues to rise, for example, that could indicate that more data would help the model perform better.

The following visualization shows a validation curve and also helps us explore bias and variance in our model (see Figure 11-2). If there is variability (a large shaded area) in the training score, then the model suffers from bias error and is too simple (underfit). If there is variability in the cross-validated score, then the model suffers from variance error and is too complicated (overfit). Another indication that the model is overfit is that the performance of the validation set is much worse than the training set.

Here is an example of creating a learning curve using Yellowbrick:

```
>>> from yellowbrick.model_selection import (
...     LearningCurve,
... )
>>> fig, ax = plt.subplots(figsize=(6, 4))
>>> lc3_viz = LearningCurve(
...     RandomForestClassifier(n_estimators=100),
...     cv=10,
... )
>>> lc3_viz.fit(X, y)
>>> lc3_viz.poof()
>>> fig.savefig("images/mlpr_1102.png", dpi=300)
```

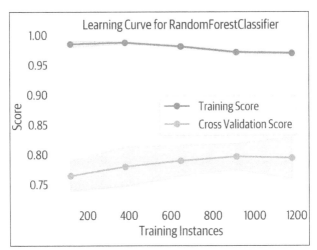

Figure 11-2. Learning curve plot. The plateau in the validation score indicates that adding more data would not improve this model.

This visualization can also be used for regression or clustering by changing the scoring options.

CHAPTER 12

Metrics and Classification Evaluation

We'll cover the following metrics and evaluation tools in this chapter: confusion matrices, various metrics, a classification report, and some visualizations.

This will be evaluated as a decision tree model that predicts Titanic survival.

Confusion Matrix

A confusion matrix can aid in understanding how a classifier performs.

A binary classifier can have four classification results: true positives (TP), true negatives (TN), false positives (FP), and false negatives (FN). The first two are correct classifications.

Here is a common example for remembering the other results. Assuming positive means pregnant and negative is not pregnant, a false positive is like claiming a man is pregnant. A false negative is claiming that a pregnant woman is not (when she is clearly showing) (see Figure 12-1). These last two types of errors are referred to as *type 1* and *type 2* errors, respectively (see Table 12-1).

Another way to remember these is that P (for false positive) has one straight line in it (type 1 error), and N (for false negative) has two vertical lines in it.

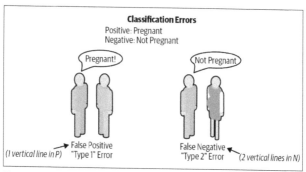

Figure 12-1. Classification errors.

Table 12-1. Binary classification results from a confusion matrix

Actual	Predicted negative	Predicted positive
Actual negative	True negative	False positive (type 1)
Actual positive	False negative (type 2)	True positive

Here is the pandas code to calculate the classification results. The comments show the results. We will use these variables to calculate other metrics:

```
>>> y_predict = dt.predict(X_test)
>>> tp = (
...     (y_test == 1) & (y_test == y_predict)
... ).sum()  # 123
>>> tn = (
...     (y_test == 0) & (y_test == y_predict)
... ).sum()  # 199
>>> fp = (
...     (y_test == 0) & (y_test != y_predict)
... ).sum()  # 25
>>> fn = (
```

```
...     (y_test == 1) & (y_test != y_predict)
... ).sum() # 46
```

Well-behaving classifiers ideally have high counts in the true diagonal. We can create a DataFrame using the sklearn confu sion_matrix function:

```
>>> from sklearn.metrics import confusion_matrix
>>> y_predict = dt.predict(X_test)
>>> pd.DataFrame(
...     confusion_matrix(y_test, y_predict),
...     columns=[
...         "Predict died",
...         "Predict Survive",
...     ],
...     index=["True Death", "True Survive"],
... )
             Predict died  Predict Survive
True Death            199               25
True Survive           46              123
```

Yellowbrick has a plot for the confusion matrix (see Figure 12-2):

```
>>> import matplotlib.pyplot as plt
>>> from yellowbrick.classifier import (
...     ConfusionMatrix,
... )
>>> mapping = {0: "died", 1: "survived"}
>>> fig, ax = plt.subplots(figsize=(6, 6))
>>> cm_viz = ConfusionMatrix(
...     dt,
...     classes=["died", "survived"],
...     label_encoder=mapping,
... )
>>> cm_viz.score(X_test, y_test)
>>> cm_viz.poof()
>>> fig.savefig("images/mlpr_1202.png", dpi=300)
```

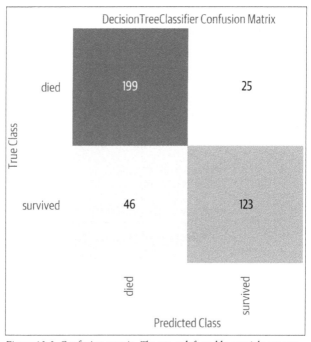

Figure 12-2. Confusion matrix. The upper left and lower right are cor-rect classifications. The lower left is false negative. The upper right is false positive.

Metrics

The `sklearn.metrics` module implements many common clas-sification metrics, including:

`'accuracy'`
    Percent of correct predictions

`'average_precision'`
    Precision recall curve summary

`'f1'`
    Harmonic mean of precision and recall

`'neg_log_loss'`

Logistic or cross-entropy loss (model must support `predict_proba`)

`'precision'`

Ability to find only relevant samples (not label a negative as a positive)

`'recall'`

Ability to find all positive samples

`'roc_auc'`

Area under the receiver operator characteristic curve

These strings can be used as the `scoring` parameter when doing grid search, or you can use functions from the `sklearn.metrics` module that have the same names as the strings but end in `_score`. See the following note for examples.

NOTE

`'f1'`, `'precision'`, and `'recall'` all support the following suffixes for multiclass classifers:

`'_micro'`

Global weighted average of metric

`'_macro'`

Unweighted average of metric

`'_weighted'`

Multiclass weighted average of metric

`'_samples'`

Per sample metric

Accuracy

Accuracy is the percentage of correct classifications:

```
>>> (tp + tn) / (tp + tn + fp + fn)
0.8142493638676844
```

What is good accuracy? It depends. If I'm predicting fraud (which usually is a rare event, say 1 in 10,000), I can get very high accuracy by always predicting not fraud. But this model is not very useful. Looking at other metrics and the cost of predicting a false positive and a false negative can help us determine if a model is decent.

We can use sklearn to calculate it for us:

```
>>> from sklearn.metrics import accuracy_score
>>> y_predict = dt.predict(X_test)
>>> accuracy_score(y_test, y_predict)
0.8142493638676844
```

Recall

Recall (also called *sensitivity*) is the percentage of positive values correctly classified. (How many relevant results are returned?)

```
>>> tp / (tp + fn)
0.7159763313609467

>>> from sklearn.metrics import recall_score
>>> y_predict = dt.predict(X_test)
>>> recall_score(y_test, y_predict)
0.7159763313609467
```

Precision

Precision is the percent of positive predictions that were correct (TP divided by (TP + FP)). (How relevant are the results?)

```
>>> tp / (tp + fp)
0.8287671232876712
```

```
>>> from sklearn.metrics import precision_score
>>> y_predict = dt.predict(X_test)
>>> precision_score(y_test, y_predict)
0.8287671232876712
```

F1

F1 is the harmonic mean of recall and precision:

```
>>> pre = tp / (tp + fp)
>>> rec = tp / (tp + fn)
>>> (2 * pre * rec) / (pre + rec)
0.7682539682539683

>>> from sklearn.metrics import f1_score
>>> y_predict = dt.predict(X_test)
>>> f1_score(y_test, y_predict)
0.7682539682539683
```

Classification Report

Yellowbrick has a classification report showing precision, recall, and f1 scores for both positive and negative values (see Figure 12-3). This is colored, and the redder the cell (closer to one), the better the score:

```
>>> import matplotlib.pyplot as plt
>>> from yellowbrick.classifier import (
...     ClassificationReport,
... )
>>> fig, ax = plt.subplots(figsize=(6, 3))
>>> cm_viz = ClassificationReport(
...     dt,
...     classes=["died", "survived"],
...     label_encoder=mapping,
... )
>>> cm_viz.score(X_test, y_test)
>>> cm_viz.poof()
>>> fig.savefig("images/mlpr_1203.png", dpi=300)
```

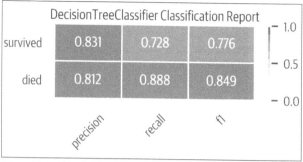

Figure 12-3. Classification report.

ROC

A ROC curve illustrates how the classifier performs by tracking the true positive rate (recall/sensitivity) as the false positive rate (inverted specificity) changes (see Figure 12-4).

A rule of thumb is that the plot should bulge out toward the top-left corner. A plot that is to the left and above another plot indicates better performance. The diagonal in this plot indicates the behavior of a random guessing classifier. By taking the AUC, you get a metric for evaluating the performance:

```
>>> from sklearn.metrics import roc_auc_score
>>> y_predict = dt.predict(X_test)
>>> roc_auc_score(y_test, y_predict)
0.8706304346418559
```

Yellowbrick can plot this for us:

```
>>> from yellowbrick.classifier import ROCAUC
>>> fig, ax = plt.subplots(figsize=(6, 6))
>>> roc_viz = ROCAUC(dt)
>>> roc_viz.score(X_test, y_test)
0.8706304346418559
>>> roc_viz.poof()
>>> fig.savefig("images/mlpr_1204.png", dpi=300)
```

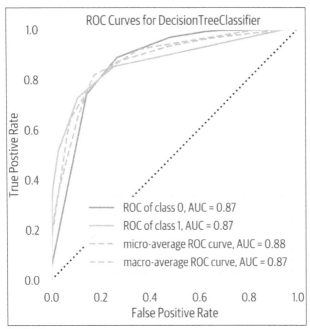

Figure 12-4. ROC curve.

Precision-Recall Curve

The ROC curve may be overly optimistic for imbalanced classes. Another option for evaluating classifiers is using a precision-recall curve (see Figure 12-5). Classification is a balancing act of finding everything you need (recall) while limiting the junk results (precision). This is typically a trade-off. As recall goes up, precision usually goes down and vice versa.

```
>>> from sklearn.metrics import (
...     average_precision_score,
... )
>>> y_predict = dt.predict(X_test)
>>> average_precision_score(y_test, y_predict)
0.7155150490642249
```

Here is a Yellowbrick precision-recall curve:

```
>>> from yellowbrick.classifier import (
...     PrecisionRecallCurve,
... )
>>> fig, ax = plt.subplots(figsize=(6, 4))
>>> viz = PrecisionRecallCurve(
...     DecisionTreeClassifier(max_depth=3)
... )
>>> viz.fit(X_train, y_train)
>>> print(viz.score(X_test, y_test))
>>> viz.poof()
>>> fig.savefig("images/mlpr_1205.png", dpi=300)
```

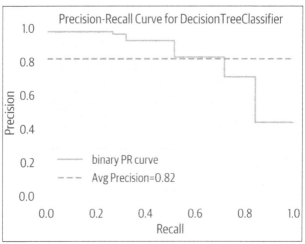

Figure 12-5. Precision-recall curve.

Cumulative Gains Plot

A cumulative gains plot can be used to evaluate a binary classifier. It models the true positive rate (sensitivity) against the
support rate (fraction of positive predictions). The intuition
behind this plot is to sort all classifications by predicted probability. Ideally there would be a clean cut that divides positive
from negative samples. If the first 10% of the predictions has
30% of the positive samples, you would plot a point from (0,0)
to (.1, .3). You continue this process through all of the samples
(see Figure 12-6).

A common use for this is determining customer response. The
cumulative gains curve plots the support or predicted positive
rate along the x-axis. Our chart labels this as "Percentage of
sample". It plots the sensitivity or true positive rate along the y-
axis. This is labeled as "Gain" in our plot.

If you wanted to contact 90% of the customers that would
respond (sensitivity), you can trace from .9 on the y-axis to the
right until you hit that curve. The x-axis at that point will indicate how many total customers you need to contact (support)
to get to 90%.

In this case we aren't contacting customers that would respond
to a survey but predicting survival on the Titanic. If we ordered
all passengers on the Titanic according to our model by how
likely they are to survive, if you took the first 65% of them, you
would have 90% of the survivors. If you have an associated cost
per contact and revenue per response, you can calculate what
the best number is.

In general, a model that is to the left and above another model
is a better model. The best models are lines that go up to the
top (if 10% of the samples are positive, it would hit at (.1, 1))
and then directly to the right. If the plot is below the baseline,
we would do better to randomly assign labels that use our
model.

The scikit-plot library (*https://oreil.ly/dg0iQ*) can create a cumulative gains plot:

```
>>> fig, ax = plt.subplots(figsize=(6, 6))
>>> y_probas = dt.predict_proba(X_test)
>>> scikitplot.metrics.plot_cumulative_gain(
...     y_test, y_probas, ax=ax
... )
>>> fig.savefig(
...     "images/mlpr_1206.png",
...     dpi=300,
...     bbox_inches="tight",
... )
```

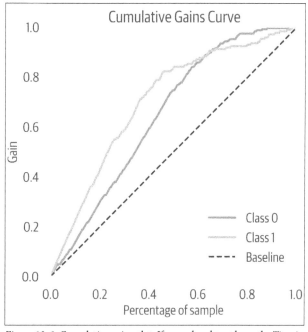

Figure 12-6. Cumulative gains plot. If we ordered people on the Titanic according to our model, looking at 20% of them we would get 40% of the survivors.

Lift Curve

A lift curve is another way of looking at the information in a cumulative gains plot. The *lift* is how much better we are doing than the baseline model. In our plot below, we can see that if we sorted our Titanic passengers by the survival probability and took the first 20% of them, our lift would be about 2.2 times (the gain divided by sample percent) better than randomly choosing survivors (see Figure 12-7). (We would get 2.2 times as many survivors.)

The scikit-plot library can create a lift curve:

```
>>> fig, ax = plt.subplots(figsize=(6, 6))
>>> y_probas = dt.predict_proba(X_test)
>>> scikitplot.metrics.plot_lift_curve(
...     y_test, y_probas, ax=ax
... )
>>> fig.savefig(
...     "images/mlpr_1207.png",
...     dpi=300,
...     bbox_inches="tight",
... )
```

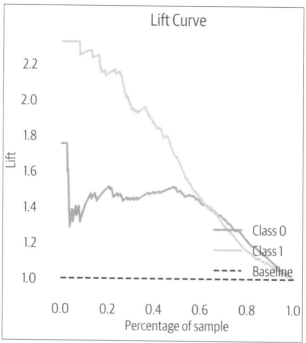

Figure 12-7. Lift curve.

Class Balance

Yellowbrick has a simple bar plot to view the class sizes. When the relative class sizes are different, accuracy is not a good evaluation metric (see Figure 12-8). When splitting up the data into training and test sets, use *stratified sampling* so the sets keep a relative proportion of the classes. (The test_train_split function does this when you set the stratify parameter to the labels.)

```
>>> from yellowbrick.classifier import ClassBalance
>>> fig, ax = plt.subplots(figsize=(6, 6))
>>> cb_viz = ClassBalance(
```

```
...         labels=["Died", "Survived"]
... )
>>> cb_viz.fit(y_test)
>>> cb_viz.poof()
>>> fig.savefig("images/mlpr_1208.png", dpi=300)
```

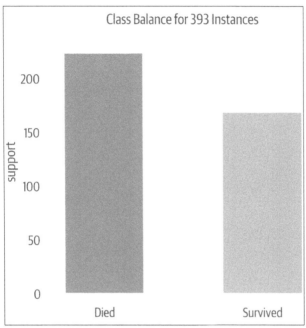

Figure 12-8. A slight class imbalance.

Class Prediction Error

The class prediction error plot from Yellowbrick is a bar chart
that visualizes a confusion matrix (see Figure 12-9):

```
>>> from yellowbrick.classifier import (
...     ClassPredictionError,
... )
>>> fig, ax = plt.subplots(figsize=(6, 3))
>>> cpe_viz = ClassPredictionError(
...     dt, classes=["died", "survived"]
... )
>>> cpe_viz.score(X_test, y_test)
>>> cpe_viz.poof()
>>> fig.savefig("images/mlpr_1209.png", dpi=300)
```

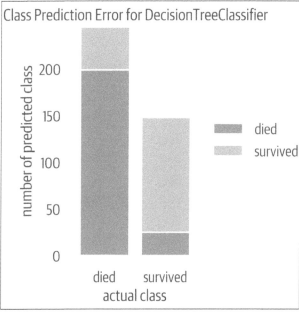

Figure 12-9. Class prediction error. At the top of the left bar are people who died, but we predicted that they survived (false positive). At the bottom of the right bar are people who survived, but the model predicted death (false negative).

Discrimination Threshold

Most binary classifiers that predict probability have a *discrimination threshold* of 50%. If the predicted probability is above 50%, the classifier assigns a positive label. Figure 12-10 moves that threshold value between 0 and 100 and shows the impact to precision, recall, f1, and queue rate.

This plot can be useful to view the trade-off between precision and recall. Assume we are looking for fraud (and considering fraud to be the positive classification). To get high recall (catch all of the fraud), we can just classify everything as fraud. But in a bank situation, this would not be profitable and would require an army of workers. To get high precision (only catch fraud if it is fraud), we could have a model that only triggers on cases of extreme fraud. But this would miss much of the fraud that might not be as obvious. There is a trade-off here.

The *queue rate* is the percent of predictions above the threshold. You can consider this to be the percent of cases to review if you are dealing with fraud.

If you have the cost for positive, negative, and erroneous calculations, you can determine what threshold you are comfortable with.

The following plot is useful to see what discrimination threshold will maximize the f1 score or adjust precision or recall to an acceptable number when coupled with the queue rate.

Yellowbrick provides this visualizer. This visualizer shuffles the data and runs 50 trials by default, splitting out 10% for validation:

```
>>> from yellowbrick.classifier import (
...      DiscriminationThreshold,
... )
>>> fig, ax = plt.subplots(figsize=(6, 5))
>>> dt_viz = DiscriminationThreshold(dt)
>>> dt_viz.fit(X, y)
>>> dt_viz.poof()
>>> fig.savefig("images/mlpr_1210.png", dpi=300)
```

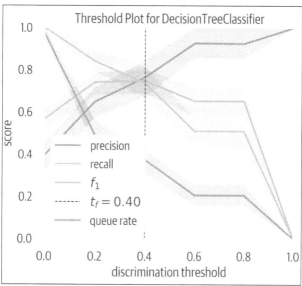

Figure 12-10. Discrimination threshold.

CHAPTER 13

Explaining Models

Predictive models have different properties. Some are designed to handle linear data. Others can mold to more complex input. Some models can be interpreted very easily, others are like black boxes and don't offer much insight into how the prediction is made.

In this chapter we will look at interpreting different models. We will look at some examples using the Titanic data.

```
>>> dt = DecisionTreeClassifier(
...     random_state=42, max_depth=3
... )
>>> dt.fit(X_train, y_train)
```

Regression Coefficients

The intercepts and regression coefficients explain the expected value, and how features impact the prediction. A positive coefficient indicates that as a feature's value increases, the prediction increases as well.

Feature Importance

Tree-based models in the scikit-learn library include a `.feature_importances_` attribute for inspecting how the features of a dataset affect the model. We can inspect or plot them.

LIME

LIME (*https://oreil.ly/shCR_*) works to help explain black-box models. It performs a *local* interpretation rather than an overall interpretation. It will help explain a single sample.

For a given data point or sample, LIME indicates which features were important in determining the result. It does this by perturbing the sample in question and fitting a linear model to it. The linear model approximates the model close to the sample (see Figure 13-1).

Here is an example explaining the last sample (which our decision tree predicts will survive) from the training data:

```
>>> from lime import lime_tabular
>>> explainer = lime_tabular.LimeTabularExplainer(
...     X_train.values,
...     feature_names=X.columns,
...     class_names=["died", "survived"],
... )
>>> exp = explainer.explain_instance(
...     X_train.iloc[-1].values, dt.predict_proba
... )
```

LIME doesn't like using DataFrames as input. Note that we converted the data to numpy arrays using `.values`.

TIP

If you are doing this in Jupyter, follow up with this code:

```
exp.show_in_notebook()
```

This will render an HTML version of the explanation.

We can create a matplotlib figure if we want to export the explanation (or aren't using Jupyter):

```
>>> fig = exp.as_pyplot_figure()
>>> fig.tight_layout()
>>> fig.savefig("images/mlpr_1301.png")
```

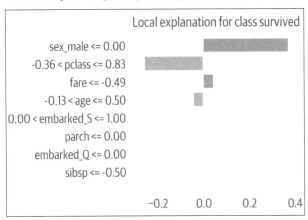

Figure 13-1. LIME explanation for the Titanic dataset. Features for the sample push the prediction toward the right (survival) or left (deceased).

Play around with this and notice that if you switch genders, the results are affected. Below we take the second to last row in the training data. The prediction for that row is 48% deceased and 52% survived. If we switch the gender, we find that the prediction shifts toward 88% deceased:

```
>>> data = X_train.iloc[-2].values.copy()
>>> dt.predict_proba(
...     [data]
... ) # predicting that a woman lives
[[0.48062016 0.51937984]]
>>> data[5] = 1 # change to male
>>> dt.predict_proba([data])
array([[0.87954545, 0.12045455]])
```

The .predict_proba method returns a probability for each label.

Tree Interpretation

For sklearn tree-based models (decision tree, random forest, and extra tree models) you can use the treeinterpreter package (*https://oreil.ly/vN1Bl*). This will calculate the bias and the contribution from each feature. The bias is the mean of the training set.

Each contribution lists how it contributes to each of the labels. (The bias plus the contributions should sum to the prediction.) Since this is a binary classification, there are only two. We see that sex_male is the most important, followed by age and fare:

```
>>> from treeinterpreter import (
...     treeinterpreter as ti,
... )
>>> instances = X.iloc[:2]
>>> prediction, bias, contribs = ti.predict(
...     rf5, instances
... )
>>> i = 0
>>> print("Instance", i)
>>> print("Prediction", prediction[i])
>>> print("Bias (trainset mean)", bias[i])
>>> print("Feature contributions:")
>>> for c, feature in zip(
...     contribs[i], instances.columns
... ):
...     print("  {} {}".format(feature, c))
Instance 0
Prediction [0.98571429 0.01428571]
Bias (trainset mean) [0.63984716 0.36015284]
Feature contributions:
  pclass [ 0.03588478 -0.03588478]
```

```
age [ 0.08569306 -0.08569306]
sibsp [ 0.01024538 -0.01024538]
parch [ 0.0100742 -0.0100742]
fare [ 0.06850243 -0.06850243]
sex_male [ 0.12000073 -0.12000073]
embarked_Q [ 0.0026364 -0.0026364]
embarked_S [ 0.01283015 -0.01283015]
```

NOTE

This example is for classification, but there is support for
regression as well.

Partial Dependence Plots

With feature importance in trees we know that a feature is
impacting the outcome, but we don't know how the impact
varies as the feature's value changes. Partial dependence plots
allow us to visualize the relation between changes in just one
feature and the outcome. We will use pdpbox (*https://oreil.ly/
O9zY2*) to visualize how age affects survival (see Figure 13-2).

This example uses a random forest model:

```
>>> rf5 = ensemble.RandomForestClassifier(
...     **{
...         "max_features": "auto",
...         "min_samples_leaf": 0.1,
...         "n_estimators": 200,
...         "random_state": 42,
...     }
... )
>>> rf5.fit(X_train, y_train)

>>> from pdpbox import pdp
>>> feat_name = "age"
>>> p = pdp.pdp_isolate(
...     rf5, X, X.columns, feat_name
... )
>>> fig, _ = pdp.pdp_plot(
...     p, feat_name, plot_lines=True
... )
>>> fig.savefig("images/mlpr_1302.png", dpi=300)
```

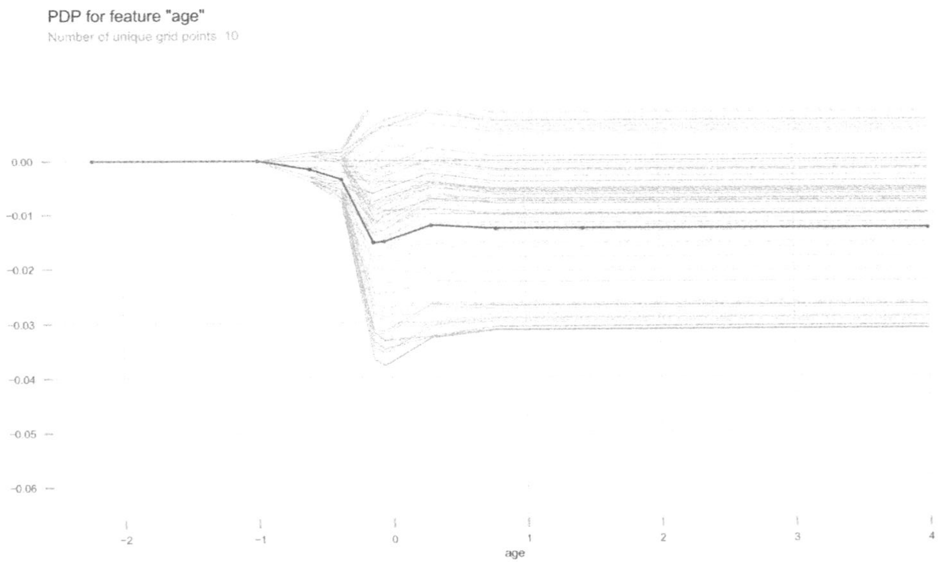
PDP for feature "age"
Number of unique grid points 10
0.00
-0.01
-0.02
-0.03
-0.04
-0.05
-0.06
-2
-1
0
1
2
3
4
age

Figure 13-2. Partial dependence plot showing what happens to the target as age changes.

We can also visualize the interactions between two features (see Figure 13-3):

```
>>> features = ["fare", "sex_male"]
>>> p = pdp.pdp_interact(
...     rf5, X, X.columns, features
... )
>>> fig, _ = pdp.pdp_interact_plot(p, features)
>>> fig.savefig("images/mlpr_1303.png", dpi=300)
```

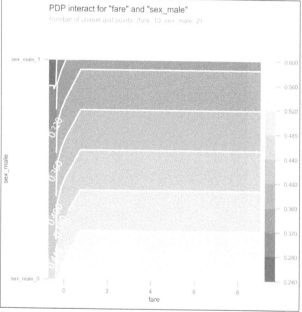

Figure 13-3. Partial dependence plot with two features. As fare goes up and sex goes from male to female, survival goes up.

Surrogate Models

If you have a model that is not interpretable (SVM or neural network), you can fit an interpretable model (decision tree) to that model. Using the surrogate you can examine the feature importances.

Here we create a Support Vector Classifier (SVC), but train a decision tree (without a depth limit to overfit and capture what is happening in this model) to explain it:

```
>>> from sklearn import svm
>>> sv = svm.SVC()
>>> sv.fit(X_train, y_train)
>>> sur_dt = tree.DecisionTreeClassifier()
>>> sur_dt.fit(X_test, sv.predict(X_test))
>>> for col, val in sorted(
...     zip(
...         X_test.columns,
...         sur_dt.feature_importances_,
...     ),
...     key=lambda x: x[1],
...     reverse=True,
... )[:7]:
...     print(f"{col:10}{val:10.3f}")
sex_male      0.723
pclass        0.076
sibsp         0.061
```

age	0.056
embarked_S	0.050
fare	0.028
parch	0.005

Shapley

The SHapley Additive exPlanations, (SHAP (*https://oreil.ly/ QYj-q*)) package can visualize feature contributions of any model. This is a really nice package because not only does it work with most models, it also can explain individual predictions and the global feature contributions.

SHAP works for both classification and regression. It generates "SHAP" values. For classification models, the SHAP value sums to log odds for binary classification. For regression, the SHAP values sum to the target prediction.

This library requires Jupyter (JavaScript) for interactivity on some of its plots. (Some can render static images with matplotlib.) Here is an example for sample 20, predicted to die:

```
>>> rf5.predict_proba(X_test.iloc[[20]])
array([[0.59223553, 0.40776447]])
```

In the force plot for sample 20, you can see the "base value." This is a female who is predicted to die (see Figure 13-4). We will use the survival index (1) because we want the right-hand side of the plot to be survival. The features push this to the right or left. The larger the feature, the more impact it has. In this case, the low fare and third class push toward death (the output value is below .5):

```
>>> import shap
>>> s = shap.TreeExplainer(rf5)
>>> shap_vals = s.shap_values(X_test)
>>> target_idx = 1
>>> shap.force_plot(
...     s.expected_value[target_idx],
...     shap_vals[target_idx][20, :],
```

```
...        feature_names=X_test.columns,
... )
```

Figure 13-4. Shapley feature contributions for sample 20. This plot shows the base value and the features that push toward death.

You can also visualize the explanations for the entire dataset (rotating them by 90 and plotting them along the x axis) (see Figure 13-5):

```
>>> shap.force_plot(
...        s.expected_value[1],
...        shap_vals[1],
...        feature_names=X_test.columns,
... )
```

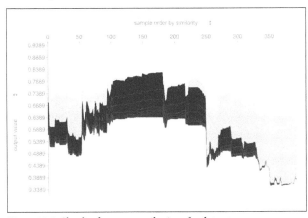

Figure 13-5. Shapley feature contributions for dataset.

The SHAP library can also generate dependence plots. The following plot (see Figure 13-6) visualizes the relationship between age and SHAP value (it is colored by pclass, which SHAP chooses automatically; specify a column name as an `interaction_index` parameter to choose your own):

```
>>> fig, ax = plt.subplots(figsize=(6, 4))
>>> res = shap.dependence_plot(
...     "age",
...     shap_vals[target_idx],
...     X_test,
...     feature_names=X_test.columns,
...     alpha=0.7,
... )
>>> fig.savefig(
...     "images/mlpr_1306.png",
...     bbox_inches="tight",
...     dpi=300,
... )
```

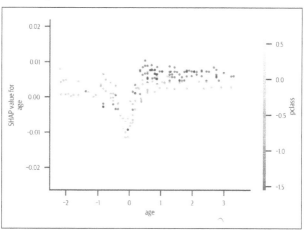

Figure 13-6. Shapley dependency plot for age. Young and old have a higher rate of survival. As age goes up, a lower pclass has more chance of survival.

In addition, we can summarize all of the features. This is a very powerful chart to understand. It shows global impact, but also individual impacts. The features are ranked by importance. The most important features are at the top.

Also the features are colored according to their value. We can see that a low sex_male score (female) has a strong push toward survival, while a high score has a less strong push toward death. The age feature is a little harder to interpret. That is because young and old values push toward survival, while middle values push toward death.

When you combine the summary plot with the dependence plot, you can get good insight into model behavior (see Figure 13-7):

```
>>> fig, ax = plt.subplots(figsize=(6, 4))
>>> shap.summary_plot(shap_vals[0], X_test)
>>> fig.savefig("images/mlpr_1307.png", dpi=300)
```

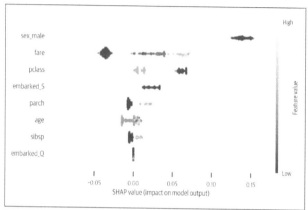

Figure 13-7. Shapley summary plot showing most important features at the top. The coloring shows how the values of the feature affect the target.

CHAPTER 14

Regression

Regression is a supervised machine learning process. It is similar to classification, but rather than predicting a label, we try to predict a continuous value. If you are trying to predict a number, then use regression.

It turns out that sklearn supports many of the same classification models for regression problems. In fact, the API is the same, calling .fit, .score, and .predict. This is also true for the next-generation boosting libraries, XGBoost and LightGBM.

Though there are similarities with the classification models and hyperparameters, the evaluation metrics are different for regression. This chapter will review many of the types of regression models. We will use the Boston housing dataset (*https://oreil.ly/b2bKQ*) to explore them.

Here we load the data, create a split version for training and testing, and create another split version with standardized data:

```
>>> import pandas as pd
>>> from sklearn.datasets import load_boston
>>> from sklearn import (
...     model_selection,
...     preprocessing,
... )
```

```
>>> b = load_boston()
>>> bos_X = pd.DataFrame(
...     b.data, columns=b.feature_names
... )
>>> bos_y = b.target

>>> bos_X_train, bos_X_test, bos_y_train,
bos_y_test = model_selection.train_test_split(
...     bos_X,
...     bos_y,
...     test_size=0.3,
...     random_state=42,
... )


>>> bos_sX = preprocessing.Stand
ardScaler().fit_transform(
...     bos_X
... )
>>> bos_sX_train, bos_sX_test, bos_sy_train,
bos_sy_test = model_selection.train_test_split(
...     bos_sX,
...     bos_y,
...     test_size=0.3,
...     random_state=42,
... )
```

Here are descriptions of the features of the housing dataset taken from the dataset:

CRIM

Per capita crime rate by town

ZN

Proportion of residential land zoned for lots over 25,000 square feet

INDUS

Proportion of nonretail business acres per town

CHAS

> Charles River dummy variable (1 if tract bounds river; 0 otherwise)

NOX

> Nitric oxides concentration (parts per 10 million)

RM

> Average number of rooms per dwelling

AGE

> Proportion of owner-occupied units built prior to 1940

DIS

> Weighted distances to five Boston employment centers

RAD

> Index of accessibility to radial highways

TAX

> Full-value property tax rate per $10,000

PTRATIO

> Pupil-teacher ratio by town

B

> $1000(Bk - 0.63)^2$, where Bk is the proportion of black people by town (this dataset is from 1978)

LSTAT

> Percent lower status of the population

MEDV

> Median value of owner-occupied homes in increments of $1000

Baseline Model

A baseline regression model will give us something to compare our other models to. In sklearn, the default result of the .score method is the *coefficient of determination* (r^2 or R^2). This number explains the percent of variation of the input data that the prediction captures. The value is typically between 0 and 1, but it can be negative in the case of particulary bad models.

The default strategy of the `DummyRegressor` is to predict the mean value of the training set. We can see that this model does not perform very well:

```
>>> from sklearn.dummy import DummyRegressor
>>> dr = DummyRegressor()
>>> dr.fit(bos_X_train, bos_y_train)
>>> dr.score(bos_X_test, bos_y_test)
-0.03469753992352409
```

Linear Regression

Simple linear regression is taught in math and beginning statistics courses. It tries to fit a form of the formula $y = mx + b$ while minimizing the square of the errors. When solved, we have an intercept and coefficient. The intercept gives a base value for a prediction modified by adding the product of the coefficient and the input.

This form can be generalized to higher dimensions. In that case each feature has a coefficient. The larger the absolute value of the coefficient, the more impact the feature has on the target.

This model assumes that the prediction is a linear combination of the inputs. For some datasets, this is not flexible enough. Complexity can be added by transforming the features (the sklearn `preprocessing.PolynomialFeatures` transformer can create polynomial combinations of the features). If this leads to overfitting, ridge and lasso regression may be used to regularize the estimator.

This model is also susceptible to *heteroscedasticity*. This is the idea that as the input values change in size, the error of the prediction (or the residuals) often changes as well. If you plot the input against the residuals, you will see a fan or cone shape. We will see examples of that later.

Another issue to be aware of is *multicollinearity*. If columns have high correlation, it can hinder interpretation of the coefficients. This usually does not impact the model, only coefficient meaning.

A linear regression model has the following properties:

Runtime efficiency
    Use n_jobs to speed up performance.

Preprocess data
    Standardize data before training the model.

Prevent overfitting
    You can simplify the model by not using or adding polynomial features.

Interpret results
    Can interpret results as weights for feature contribution, but assumes normality and independence of features. You might want to remove colinear features to improve interpretability. R^2 will tell you how much of the total variance of the outcome is explained by the model.

Here is a sample run with the default data:

```
>>> from sklearn.linear_model import (
...     LinearRegression,
... )
>>> lr = LinearRegression()
>>> lr.fit(bos_X_train, bos_y_train)
LinearRegression(copy_X=True, fit_intercept=True,
  n_jobs=1, normalize=False)
>>> lr.score(bos_X_test, bos_y_test)
0.7109203586326287
>>> lr.coef_
array([-1.32774155e-01,  3.57812335e-02,
   4.99454423e-02,  3.12127706e+00,
  -1.54698463e+01,  4.04872721e+00,
  -1.07515901e-02, -1.38699758e+00,
   2.42353741e-01, -8.69095363e-03,
```

```
         -9.11917342e-01,  1.19435253e-02,
         -5.48080157e-01])
```

Instance parameters:

```
n_jobs=None
```
    Number of CPUs to use. -1 is all.

Attributes after fitting:

```
coef_
```
    Linear regression coefficients

```
intercept_
```
    Intercept of the linear model

The .intercept_ value is the expected mean value. You can see how scaling the data affects the coefficients. The sign of the coefficients explains the direction of the relation between the feature and the target. A positive sign indicates that as the feature increases, the label increases. A negative sign indicates that as the feature increases, the label decreases. The larger the absolute value of the coefficient, the more impact it has:

```
>>> lr2 = LinearRegression()
>>> lr2.fit(bos_sX_train, bos_sy_train)
LinearRegression(copy_X=True, fit_intercept=True,
  n_jobs=1, normalize=False)
>>> lr2.score(bos_sX_test, bos_sy_test)
0.7109203586326278
>>> lr2.intercept_
22.50945471291039
>>> lr2.coef_
array([-1.14030209,  0.83368112,  0.34230461,
   0.792002, -1.7908376, 2.84189278, -0.30234582,
   -2.91772744,  2.10815064, -1.46330017,
   -1.97229956,  1.08930453, -3.91000474])
```

You can use Yellowbrick to visualize coefficients (see Figure 14-1). Because the scaled Boston data is a numpy array rather than a pandas DataFrame, we need to pass the labels parameter if we want to use the column names:

```
>>> from yellowbrick.features import (
...     FeatureImportances,
... )
>>> fig, ax = plt.subplots(figsize=(6, 4))
>>> fi_viz = FeatureImportances(
...     lr2, labels=bos_X.columns
... )
>>> fi_viz.fit(bos_sX, bos_sy)
>>> fi_viz.poof()
>>> fig.savefig(
...     "images/mlpr_1401.png",
...     bbox_inches="tight",
...     dpi=300,
... )
```

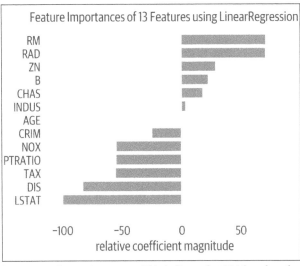

Figure 14-1. Feature importance. This indicates that RM (number of rooms) increases the price, age doesn't really matter, and LSTAT (percent of low status in population) lowers the price.

SVMs

Support vector machines can perform regression as well.

SVMs have the following properties:

Runtime efficiency

The scikit-learn implementation is $O(n^4)$, so it can be hard to scale to large sizes. Using a linear kernel or the Line arSVR model can improve the runtime performance at perhaps the cost of accuracy. Upping the cache_size parameter can bring that down to $O(n^3)$.

Preprocess data

The algorithm is not scale invariant, so standardizing the data is highly recommended.

Prevent overfitting

The C (penalty parameter) controls regularization. A smaller value allows for a smaller margin in the hyperplane. A higher value for gamma will tend to overfit the training data. The LinearSVR model supports a loss and penalty parameter for regularization. The epsilon parameter can be raised (with 0 you should expect overfitting).

Interpret results

Inspect .support_vectors_, though these are hard to interpret. With linear kernels, you can inspect .coef_.

Here is an example of using the library:

```
>>> from sklearn.svm import SVR
>>> svr = SVR()
>>> svr.fit(bos_sX_train, bos_sy_train)
SVR(C=1.0, cache_size=200, coef0=0.0, degree=3,
  epsilon=0.1, gamma='auto', kernel='rbf',
  max_iter=-1, shrinking=True, tol=0.001,
  verbose=False)

>>> svr.score(bos_sX_test, bos_sy_test)
0.6555356362002485
```

Instance parameters:

`C=1.0`
> The penalty parameter. The smaller the value, the tighter the decision boundary (more overfitting).

`cache_size=200`
> Cache size (MB). Bumping this up can improve training time on large datasets.

`coef0=0.0`
> Independent term for poly and sigmoid kernels.

`epsilon=0.1`
> Defines a margin of tolerance where no penalty is given to errors. Should be smaller for larger datasets.

`degree=3`
> Degree for polynomial kernel.

`gamma='auto'`
> Kernel coefficient. Can be a number, `'scale'` (default in 0.22, 1 / (`num features * X.std()`)), or `'auto'` (default prior, 1 / `num_features`). A lower value leads to overfitting the training data.

`kernel='rbf'`
> Kernel type: `'linear'`, `'poly'`, `'rbf'` (default), `'sigmoid'`, `'precomputed'`, or a function.

`max_iter=-1`
> Maximum number of iterations for solver. -1 for no limit.

`probability=False`
> Enable probability estimation. Slows down training.

`random_state=None`
> Random seed.

`shrinking=True`
> Use shrinking heuristic.

`tol=0.001`
> Stopping tolerance.

```
verbose=False
```
> Verbosity.

Attributes after fitting:

```
support_
```
> Support vector indices

```
support_vectors_
```
> Support vectors

```
coef_
```
> Coefficients (for linear) kernel

```
intercept_
```
> Constant for decision function

K-Nearest Neighbor

The KNN model also supports regression by finding k neighbor targets to the sample for which you want to predict. For regression, this model averages the targets together to determine a prediction.

Nearest neighbor models have the following properties:

Runtime efficiency
> Training runtime is O(1), but there is a trade-off as the sample data needs to be stored. Testing runtime is O(Nd), where N is the number of training examples and d is dimensionality.

Preprocess data
> Yes, distance-based calculations perform better when standardized.

Prevent overfitting
> Raise n_neighbors. Change p for L1 or L2 metric.

Interpret results
> Interpret the k-nearest neighbors to the sample (using the .kneighbors method). Those neighbors (if you can explain them) explain your result.

Here is an example of using the model:

```
>>> from sklearn.neighbors import (
...     KNeighborsRegressor,
... )
>>> knr = KNeighborsRegressor()
>>> knr.fit(bos_sX_train, bos_sy_train)
KNeighborsRegressor(algorithm='auto',
  leaf_size=30, metric='minkowski',
  metric_params=None, n_jobs=1, n_neighbors=5,
  p=2, weights='uniform')

>>> knr.score(bos_sX_test, bos_sy_test)
0.747112767457727
```

Attributes:

`algorithm='auto'`
    Can be `'brute'`, `'ball_tree'`, or `'kd_tree'`.

`leaf_size=30`
    Used for tree algorithms.

`metric='minkowski'`
    Distance metric.

`metric_params=None`
    Additional dictionary of parameters for custom metric function.

`n_jobs=1`
    Number of CPUs.

`n_neighbors=5`
    Number of neighbors.

`p=2`
    Minkowski power parameter. 1 = manhattan (L1). 2 = euclidean (L2).

`weights='uniform'`
    Can be `'distance'`, in which case, closer points have more influence.

Decision Tree

Decision trees support classification and regression. At each level of the tree, various splits on features are evaluated. The split that will produce the lowest error (impurity) is chosen. The `criterion` parameter can be adjusted to determine the metric for impurity.

Decision trees have the following properties:

Runtime efficiency
> For creation, loop over each of the m features we have to sort all n samples: O(mn log n). For predicting, you walk the tree: O(height).

Preprocess data
> Scaling not necessary. Need to get rid of missing values and convert to numeric.

Prevent overfitting
> Set `max_depth` to a lower number, raise `min_impurity_decrease`.

Interpret results
> Can step through the tree of choices. Because there are steps, a tree is bad at dealing with linear relationships (a small change in the values of a feature can cause a completely different tree to be formed). The tree is also highly dependent on the training data. A small change can change the whole tree.

Here is an example using the scikit-learn library:

```
>>> from sklearn.tree import DecisionTreeRegressor
>>> dtr = DecisionTreeRegressor(random_state=42)
>>> dtr.fit(bos_X_train, bos_y_train)
DecisionTreeRegressor(criterion='mse',
  max_depth=None, max_features=None,
  max_leaf_nodes=None, min_impurity_decrease=0.0,
  min_impurity_split=None, min_samples_leaf=1,
  min_samples_split=2,
  min_weight_fraction_leaf=0.0, presort=False,
```

```
        random_state=42, splitter='best')

    >>> dtr.score(bos_X_test, bos_y_test)
    0.8426751288675483
```

Instance parameters:

`criterion='mse'`

Splitting function. Default is mean squared error (L2 loss). `'friedman_mse'` or `'mae'` (L1 loss).

`max_depth=None`

Depth of tree. Default will build until leaves contain less than `min_samples_split`.

`max_features=None`

Number of features to examine for split. Default is all.

`max_leaf_nodes=None`

Limit number of leaves. Default is unlimited.

`min_impurity_decrease=0.0`

Split node if a split will decrease impurity >= value.

`min_impurity_split=None`

Deprecated.

`min_samples_leaf=1`

Minimum number of samples at each leaf.

`min_samples_split=2`

Minimum number of samples required to split a node.

`min_weight_fraction_leaf=0.0`

Minimum sum of weights required for leaf nodes.

`presort=False`

May speed up training with small dataset or restricted depth if set to `True`.

`random_state=None`

Random seed.

```
splitter='best'
    Use 'random' or 'best'.
```

Attributes after fitting:

```
feature_importances_
    Array of Gini importance
```

```
max_features_
    Computed value of max_features
```

```
n_outputs_
    Number of outputs
```

```
n_features_
    Number of features
```

```
tree_
    Underlying tree object
```

View the tree (see Figure 14-2):

```
>>> import pydotplus
>>> from io import StringIO
>>> from sklearn.tree import export_graphviz
>>> dot_data = StringIO()
>>> tree.export_graphviz(
...     dtr,
...     out_file=dot_data,
...     feature_names=bos_X.columns,
...     filled=True,
... )
>>> g = pydotplus.graph_from_dot_data(
...     dot_data.getvalue()
... )
>>> g.write_png("images/mlpr_1402.png")
```

For Jupyter, use:

```
from IPython.display import Image
Image(g.create_png())
```

Figure 14-2. Decision tree.

This plot was a little wide. On a computer you can zoom in on portions of it. You can also limit the depth of the chart (see Figure 14-3). (It turns out that the most important features are typically near the top of the tree.) We will use the max_depth parameter to do this:

```
>>> dot_data = StringIO()
>>> tree.export_graphviz(
...     dtr,
...     max_depth=2,
...     out_file=dot_data,
...     feature_names=bos_X.columns,
...     filled=True,
... )
>>> g = pydotplus.graph_from_dot_data(
...     dot_data.getvalue()
... )
>>> g.write_png("images/mlpr_1403.png")
```

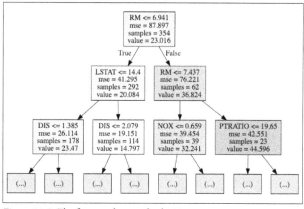

Figure 14-3. The first two layers of a decision tree.

We can also use the dtreeviz package to view a scatter plot at each of the nodes of the tree (see Figure 14-4). We will use a tree limited to a depth of two so we can see the details:

```
>>> dtr3 = DecisionTreeRegressor(max_depth=2)
>>> dtr3.fit(bos_X_train, bos_y_train)
>>> viz = dtreeviz.trees.dtreeviz(
...     dtr3,
...     bos_X,
...     bos_y,
...     target_name="price",
...     feature_names=bos_X.columns,
... )
>>> viz
```

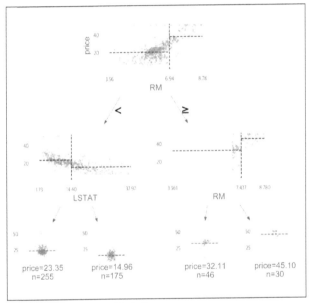

Figure 14-4. Regression with dtviz.

Feature importance:

```
>>> for col, val in sorted(
...     zip(
...         bos_X.columns, dtr.feature_importances_
...     ),
...     key=lambda x: x[1],
```

```
...       reverse=True,
... )[:5]:
...       print(f"{col:10}{val:10.3f}")
RM            0.574
LSTAT         0.191
DIS           0.110
CRIM          0.061
RAD           0.018
```

Random Forest

Decision trees are good because they are explainable, but they have a tendency to overfit. A random forest trades some of the explainability for a model that tends to generalize better. This model can also be used for regression.

Random forests have the following properties:

Runtime efficiency
> Need to create j random trees. This can be done in parallel using n_jobs. Complexity for each tree is O(mn log n), where n is the number of samples and m is the number of features. For creation, loop over each of the m features, and sort all n samples: O(mn log n). For predicting, you walk the tree: O(height).

Preprocess data
> Not necessary as long as the input is numeric and not missing values.

Prevent overfitting
> Add more trees (n_estimators). Use lower max_depth.

Interpret results
> Supports feature importance, but we don't have a single decision tree that we can walk through. Can inspect single trees from the ensemble.

Here is an example of using the model:

```
>>> from sklearn.ensemble import (
...       RandomForestRegressor,
```

```
    ... )
    >>> rfr = RandomForestRegressor(
    ...      random_state=42, n_estimators=100
    ... )
    >>> rfr.fit(bos_X_train, bos_y_train)
    RandomForestRegressor(bootstrap=True,
      criterion='mse', max_depth=None,
      max_features='auto', max_leaf_nodes=None,
      min_impurity_decrease=0.0,
      min_impurity_split=None,_samples_leaf=1,
      min_samples_split=2,
      min_weight_fraction_leaf=0.0,
      n_estimators=100, n_jobs=1,
      oob_score=False, random_state=42,
      verbose=0, warm_start=False)

    >>> rfr.score(bos_X_test, bos_y_test)
    0.8641887615545837
```

Instance parameters (these options mirror the decision tree):

bootstrap=True
    Bootstrap when building trees.

criterion='mse'
    Splitting function, 'mae'.

max_depth=None
    Depth of tree. Default will build until leaves contain less
    than min_samples_split.

max_features='auto'
    Number of features to examine for split. Default is all.

max_leaf_nodes=None
    Limit number of leaves. Default is unlimited.

min_impurity_decrease=0.0
    Split node if a split will decrease impurity by this value or
    more.

min_impurity_split=None
    Deprecated.

```
min_samples_leaf=1
```
Minimum number of samples at each leaf.

```
min_samples_split=2
```
Minimum number of samples required to split a node.

```
min_weight_fraction_leaf=0.0
```
Minimum sum total of weights required for leaf nodes.

```
n_estimators=10
```
Number of trees in the forest.

```
n_jobs=None
```
Number of jobs for fitting and predicting. (None means 1.)

```
oob_score=False
```
Whether to use OOB samples to estimate score on unseen data.

```
random_state=None
```
Random seed.

```
verbose=0
```
Verbosity.

```
warm_start=False
```
Fit a new forest or use existing one.

Attributes after fitting:

```
estimators_
```
Collection of trees

```
feature_importances_
```
Array of Gini importance

```
n_classes_
```
Number of classes

```
n_features_
```
Number of features

```
oob_score_
```
Score of the training dataset using OOB estimate

Feature importance:

```
>>> for col, val in sorted(
...     zip(
...         bos_X.columns, rfr.feature_importances_
...     ),
...     key=lambda x: x[1],
...     reverse=True,
... )[:5]:
...     print(f"{col:10}{val:10.3f}")
RM            0.505
LSTAT         0.283
DIS           0.115
CRIM          0.029
PTRATIO       0.016
```

XGBoost Regression

The XGBoost library also supports regression. It builds a simple decision tree, then "boosts" it by adding subsequent trees. Each tree tries to correct the residuals of the previous output. In practice, this works quite well on structured data.

It has the following properties:

Runtime efficiency
> XGBoost is parallelizeable. Use the n_jobs option to indicate the number of CPUs. Use GPU for even better performance.

Preprocess data
> No scaling necessary with tree models. Need to encode categorical data. Supports missing data!

Prevent overfitting
> The early_stopping_rounds=N parameter can be set to stop training if there is no improvement after N rounds. L1 and L2 regularization are controlled by reg_alpha and reg_lambda, respectively. Higher numbers mean more conservative.

Interpret results

　　Has feature importance.

Here is an example using the library:

```
>>> xgr = xgb.XGBRegressor(random_state=42)
>>> xgr.fit(bos_X_train, bos_y_train)
XGBRegressor(base_score=0.5, booster='gbtree',
  colsample_bylevel=1, colsample_bytree=1,
  gamma=0, learning_rate=0.1, max_delta_step=0,
  max_depth=3, min_child_weight=1, missing=None,
  n_estimators=100, n_jobs=1, nthread=None,
  objective='reg:linear', random_state=42,
  reg_alpha=0, reg_lambda=1, scale_pos_weight=1,
  seed=None, silent=True, subsample=1)

>>> xgr.score(bos_X_test, bos_y_test)
0.871679473122472

>>> xgr.predict(bos_X.iloc[[0]])
array([27.013563], dtype=float32)
```

Instance parameters:

`max_depth=3`
　　Maximum depth.

`learning_rate=0.1`
　　Learning rate (eta) for boosting (between 0 and 1). After
　　each boost step, the newly added weights are scaled by this
　　factor. The lower the value, the more conservative, but will
　　also need more trees to converge. In the call to `.train`, you
　　can pass a `learning_rates` parameter, which is a list of
　　rates at each round (i.e., `[.1]*100 + [.05]*100`).

`n_estimators=100`
　　Number of rounds or boosted trees.

`silent=True`
　　Whether to print messages while running boosting.

`objective="reg:linear"`
　　Learning task or callable for classification.

`booster="gbtree"`
    Can be `'gbtree'`, `'gblinear'`, or `'dart'`. The `'dart'` option adds dropout (drops random trees to prevent overfitting). The `'gblinear'` option creates a regularized linear model (read not a tree but similar to lasso regression).

`nthread=None`
    Deprecated.

`n_jobs=1`
    Number of threads to use.

`gamma=0`
    Minimum loss reduction needed to further split a leaf.

`min_child_weight=1`
    Minimum value for sum of hessian for a child.

`max_delta_step=0`
    Make update more conservative. Set 1 to 10 for imbalanced classes.

`subsample=1`
    Fraction of samples to use for next boosting round.

`colsample_bytree=1`
    Fraction of columns to use for boosting round.

`colsample_bylevel=1`
    Fraction of columns to use for level in tree.

`colsample_bynode=1`
    Fraction of columns to use for split (node in tree).

`reg_alpha=0`
    L1 regularization (mean of weights). Increase to be more conservative.

`reg_lambda=1`
    L2 regularization (root of squared weights). Increase to be more conservative.

`base_score=.5`
    Initial prediction.

```
seed=None
    Deprecated.
```

```
random_state=0
    Random seed.
```

```
missing=None
    Value to interpret for missing. None means np.nan.
```

```
importance_type='gain'
    The feature importance type: 'gain', 'weight', 'cover',
    'total_gain', or 'total_cover'.
```

Attributes:

```
coef_
    Coefficients for gblinear learners (booster = 'gblinear')
```

```
intercept_
    Intercept for gblinear learners
```

```
feature_importances_
    Feature importances for gbtree learners
```

Feature importance is the average gain across all the nodes
where the feature is used:

```
>>> for col, val in sorted(
...     zip(
...         bos_X.columns, xgr.feature_importances_
...     ),
...     key=lambda x: x[1],
...     reverse=True,
... )[:5]:
...     print(f"{col:10}{val:10.3f}")
DIS           0.187
CRIM          0.137
RM            0.137
LSTAT         0.134
AGE           0.110
```

XGBoost includes plotting facilities for feature importance.
Note that the importance_type parameter changes the values in

---

this plot (see Figure 14-5). The default is using weight to determine feature importance:

```
>>> fig, ax = plt.subplots(figsize=(6, 4))
>>> xgb.plot_importance(xgr, ax=ax)
>>> fig.savefig("images/mlpr_1405.png", dpi=300)
```

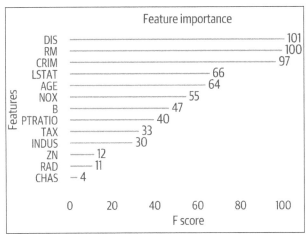

Figure 14-5. Feature importance using weight (how many times a feature is split on in the trees).

Using Yellowbrick to plot feature importances (it will normalize the feature_importances_ attribute) (see Figure 14-6):

```
>>> fig, ax = plt.subplots(figsize=(6, 4))
>>> fi_viz = FeatureImportances(xgr)
>>> fi_viz.fit(bos_X_train, bos_y_train)
>>> fi_viz.poof()
>>> fig.savefig("images/mlpr_1406.png", dpi=300)
```

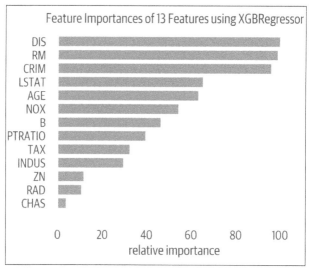

Figure 14-6. Feature importance using relative importance of gain (percent importance of the most important feature).

XGBoost provides both a textual representation of the trees and a graphical one. Here is the text representation:

```
>>> booster = xgr.get_booster()
>>> print(booster.get_dump()[0])
0:[LSTAT<9.72500038] yes=1,no=2,missing=1
  1:[RM<6.94099998] yes=3,no=4,missing=3
    3:[DIS<1.48494995] yes=7,no=8,missing=7
      7:leaf=3.9599998
      8:leaf=2.40158272
    4:[RM<7.43700027] yes=9,no=10,missing=9
      9:leaf=3.22561002
      10:leaf=4.31580687
  2:[LSTAT<16.0849991] yes=5,no=6,missing=5
    5:[B<116.024994] yes=11,no=12,missing=11
      11:leaf=1.1825
      12:leaf=1.99701393
    6:[NOX<0.603000045] yes=13,no=14,missing=13
```

```
13:leaf=1.6868
14:leaf=1.18572915
```

The leaf values can be interpreted as the sum of the `base_score` and the leaf. (To validate this, call `.predict` with the `ntree_limit=1` parameter to limit the model to using the result of the first tree.)

Here is a graphical version of the tree (see Figure 14-7):

```
fig, ax = plt.subplots(figsize=(6, 4))
xgb.plot_tree(xgr, ax=ax, num_trees=0)
fig.savefig('images/mlpr_1407.png', dpi=300)
```

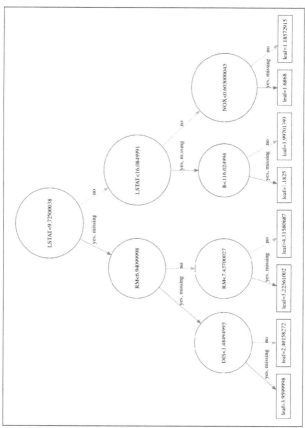

Figure 14-7. XGBoost tree.

LightGBM Regression

The gradient boosting tree library, LightGBM, also supports regression. As mentioned in the classification chapter, it can be faster than XGBoost for creating trees due to the sampling mechanism used to determine node splits.

Also, remember that it grows trees depth first, so limiting depth may harm the model. It has the following properties:

Runtime efficiency
> Can take advantage of multiple CPUs. By using binning, can be 15 times faster than XGBoost.

Preprocess data
> Has some support for encoding categorical columns as integers (or pandas `Categorical` type), but AUC appears to suffer compared to one-hot encoding.

Prevent overfitting
> Lower `num_leaves`. Increase `min_data_in_leaf`. Use `min_gain_to_split` with `lambda_l1` or `lambda_l2`.

Interpret results
> Feature importance is available. Individual trees are weak and tend to be hard to interpret.

Here is an example of using the model:

```
>>> import lightgbm as lgb
>>> lgr = lgb.LGBMRegressor(random_state=42)
>>> lgr.fit(bos_X_train, bos_y_train)
LGBMRegressor(boosting_type='gbdt',
  class_weight=None, colsample_bytree=1.0,
  learning_rate=0.1, max_depth=-1,
  min_child_samples=20, min_child_weight=0.001,
  min_split_gain=0.0, n_estimators=100,
  n_jobs=-1, num_leaves=31, objective=None,
  random_state=42, reg_alpha=0.0,
  reg_lambda=0.0, silent=True, subsample=1.0,
  subsample_for_bin=200000, subsample_freq=0)

>>> lgr.score(bos_X_test, bos_y_test)
0.847729219534575

>>> lgr.predict(bos_X.iloc[[0]])
array([30.31689569])
```

Instance parameters:

`boosting_type='gbdt'`
> Can be `'gbdt'` (gradient boosting), `'rf'` (random forest), `'dart'` (dropouts meet multiple additive regression trees), or `'goss'` (gradient-based, one-sided sampling).

`num_leaves=31`
> Maximum tree leaves.

`max_depth=-1`
> Maximum tree depth. -1 is unlimited. Larger depths tend to overfit more.

`learning_rate=0.1`
> Range (0, 1.0]. Learning rate for boosting. A smaller value slows down overfitting as the boosting rounds have less impact. A smaller number should give better performance but will require more `num_iterations`.

`n_estimators=100`
> Number of trees or boosting rounds.

`subsample_for_bin=200000`
> Samples required to create bins.

`objective=None`
> None - Does regression by default. Can be a function or string.

`min_split_gain=0.0`
> Loss reduction required to partition leaf.

`min_child_weight=0.001`
> Sum of hessian weight required for a leaf. Larger will be more conservative.

`min_child_samples=20`
> Number of samples required for a leaf. Lower numbers mean more overfitting.

`subsample=1.0`
> Fraction of samples to use for the next round.

`subsample_freq=0`

Subsample frequency. Change to 1 to enable.

`colsample_bytree=1.0`

Range (0, 1.0]. Select percent of features for each boosting round.

`reg_alpha=0.0`

L1 regularization (mean of weights). Increase to be more conservative.

`reg_lambda=0.0`

L2 regularization (root of squared weights). Increase to be more conservative.

`random_state=42`

Random seed.

`n_jobs=-1`

Number of threads.

`silent=True`

Verbose mode.

`importance_type='split'`

Determines how importance is calculated: *split* (times a feature was used) or *gain* (total gains of splits when a feature was used).

LightGBM supports feature importance. The `importance_type` parameter determines how this is calculated (the default is based on how many times a feature was used):

```
>>> for col, val in sorted(
...     zip(
...         bos_X.columns, lgr.feature_importances_
...     ),
...     key=lambda x: x[1],
...     reverse=True,
... )[:5]:
...     print(f"{col:10}{val:10.3f}")
LSTAT       226.000
RM          199.000
```

DIS	172.000
AGE	130.000
B	121.000

Feature importance plot showing how many times a feature is used (see Figure 14-8):

```
>>> fig, ax = plt.subplots(figsize=(6, 4))
>>> lgb.plot_importance(lgr, ax=ax)
>>> fig.tight_layout()
>>> fig.savefig("images/mlpr_1408.png", dpi=300)
```

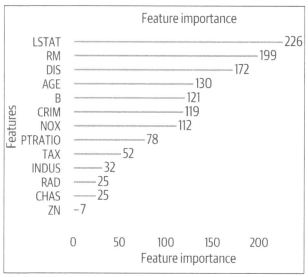

Figure 14-8. Feature importance showing how many times a feature is used.

TIP

In Jupyter, use the following command to view a tree:

```
lgb.create_tree_digraph(lgbr)
```

CHAPTER 15

Metrics and Regression Evaluation

This chapter will evaluate the results of a random forest regressor trained on the Boston housing data:

```
>>> rfr = RandomForestRegressor(
...     random_state=42, n_estimators=100
... )
>>> rfr.fit(bos_X_train, bos_y_train)
```

Metrics

The `sklearn.metrics` module includes metrics to evaluate regression models. Metric functions ending in `loss` or `error` should be minimized. Functions ending in `score` should be maximized.

The *coefficient of determination* (r^2) is a common regression metric. This value is typically between 0 and 1. It represents the percent of the variance of the target that the features contribute. Higher values are better, but in general it is difficult to evaluate the model from this metric alone. Does a .7 mean it is a good score? It depends. For a given dataset, .5 might be a good score, while for another dataset, a .9 may be a bad score. Typically we use this number in combination with other metrics or visualizations to evaluate a model.

For example, it is easy to make a model that predicts stock prices for the next day with an r^2 of .99. But I wouldn't trade my own money with that model. It might be slightly low or high, which can wreak havoc on trades.

The r^2 metric is the default metric used during grid search. You can specify other metrics using the `scoring` parameter.

The `.score` method calculates this for regression models:

```
>>> from sklearn import metrics
>>> rfr.score(bos_X_test, bos_y_test)
0.8721182042634867

>>> metrics.r2_score(bos_y_test, bos_y_test_pred)
0.8721182042634867
```

NOTE

There is also an *explained variance* metric (`'explained_variance'` in grid search). If the mean of the *residuals* (errors in predictions) is 0 (in ordinary least squares (OLS) models), then the variance explained is the same as the coefficient of determination:

```
>>> metrics.explained_variance_score(
...         bos_y_test, bos_y_test_pred
... )
0.8724890451227875
```

Mean absolute error (`'neg_mean_absolute_error'` when used in grid search) expresses the average absolute model prediction error. A perfect model would score 0, but this metric has no upper bounds, unlike the coefficient of determination. However, since it is in units of the target, it is more interpretable. If you want to ignore outliers, this is a good metric to use.

This measure cannot indicate how bad a model is, but can be used to compare two models. If you have two models, the model with a lower score is better.

This number tells us that the average error is about two above or below the real value:

```
>>> metrics.mean_absolute_error(
...     bos_y_test, bos_y_test_pred
... )
2.0839802631578945
```

Root mean squared error ('neg_mean_squared_error' in grid search) also measures model error in terms of the target. However, because it averages the square of errors before taking the square root, it penalizes large errors. If you want to penalize large errors, this is a good metric to use. For example, if being off by eight is more than two times worse than being off by four.

As with mean absolute error, this measure cannot indicate how bad a model is, but can be used to compare two models. If you assume that errors are normally distributed, this is a good choice.

The result tells us if we square the errors and average them, the result will be around 9.5:

```
>>> metrics.mean_squared_error(
...     bos_y_test, bos_y_test_pred
... )
9.52886846710526
```

The *mean squared logarithmic error* (in grid search, 'neg_mean_squared_log_error') penalizes underprediction more than overprediction. If you have targets that experience exponential growth (population, stock, etc.), this is a good metric.

If you take the log of the error and then square it, the average of these results will be 0.021:

```
>>> metrics.mean_squared_log_error(
...     bos_y_test, bos_y_test_pred
... )
0.02128263061776433
```

Residuals Plot

Good models (with appropriate R2 scores) will exhibit *homoscedasticity*. This means the variance is the same for all values of targets regardless of the input. Plotted, this looks like randomly distributed values in a residuals plot. If there are patterns, the model or the data are problematic.

Residuals plots also show outliers, which can have a big impact on model fitting (see Figure 15-1).

Yellowbrick can make residuals plots to visualize this:

```
>>> from yellowbrick.regressor import ResidualsPlot
>>> fig, ax = plt.subplots(figsize=(6, 4))
>>> rpv = ResidualsPlot(rfr)
>>> rpv.fit(bos_X_train, bos_y_train)
>>> rpv.score(bos_X_test, bos_y_test)
>>> rpv.poof()
>>> fig.savefig("images/mlpr_1501.png", dpi=300)
```

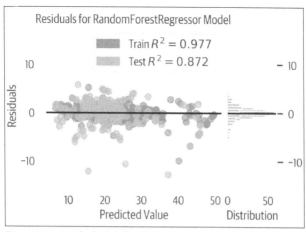

Figure 15-1. Residuals plot. Further testing will show these to be heteroscedastic.

Heteroscedasticity

The statsmodel library (*https://oreil.ly/HtIi5*) includes the *Breusch-Pagan test* for heteroscedasticity. This means that variance of the residuals varies over the predicted values. In the Breusch-Pagan test, if the p-values are significant (p-value less than 0.05), the null hypothesis of homoscedasticity is rejected. This indicates that residuals are heteroscedastic, and the predictions are biased.

The test confirms heteroscedasticity:

```
>>> import statsmodels.stats.api as sms
>>> hb = sms.het_breuschpagan(resids, bos_X_test)
>>> labels = [
...     "Lagrange multiplier statistic",
...     "p-value",
...     "f-value",
...     "f p-value",
... ]
>>> for name, num in zip(name, hb):
```

```
...         print(f"{name}: {num:.2}")
Lagrange multiplier statistic: 3.6e+01
p-value: 0.00036
f-value: 3.3
f p-value: 0.00022
```

Normal Residuals

The scipy library includes a *probability plot* and the *Kolmogorov-Smirnov test*, both of which measure whether the residuals are normal.

We can plot a histogram (see Figure 15-2) to visualize the residuals and check for normality:

```
>>> fig, ax = plt.subplots(figsize=(6, 4))
>>> resids = bos_y_test - rfr.predict(bos_X_test)
>>> pd.Series(resids, name="residuals").plot.hist(
...         bins=20, ax=ax, title="Residual Histogram"
... )
>>> fig.savefig("images/mlpr_1502.png", dpi=300)
```

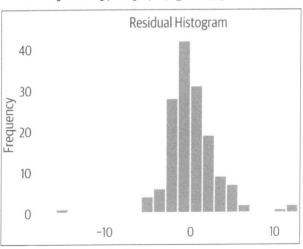

Figure 15-2. Histogram of residuals.

Figure 15-3 shows a probability plot. If the samples plotted against the quantiles line up, the residuals are normal. We can see that this fails in this case:

```
>>> from scipy import stats
>>> fig, ax = plt.subplots(figsize=(6, 4))
>>> _ = stats.probplot(resids, plot=ax)
>>> fig.savefig("images/mlpr_1503.png", dpi=300)
```

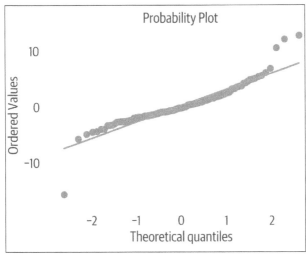

Figure 15-3. Probability plot of residuals.

The Kolmogorov-Smirnov test can evaluate whether a distribution is normal. If the p-value is significant (< 0.05), then the values are not normal.

This fails as well, which tells us the residuals are not normal:

```
>>> stats.kstest(resids, cdf="norm")
KstestResult(statistic=0.1962230021010155,
pvalue=1.3283596864921421e-05)
```

Prediction Error Plot

A prediction error plot shows the real targets against the predicted values. For a perfect model these points would line up in a 45-degree line.

As our model seems to predict lower values for the high end of y, the model has some performance issues. This is also evident in the residuals plot (see Figure 15-4).

Here is the Yellowbrick version:

```
>>> from yellowbrick.regressor import (
...     PredictionError,
... )
>>> fig, ax = plt.subplots(figsize=(6, 6))
>>> pev = PredictionError(rfr)
>>> pev.fit(bos_X_train, bos_y_train)
>>> pev.score(bos_X_test, bos_y_test)
>>> pev.poof()
>>> fig.savefig("images/mlpr_1504.png", dpi=300)
```

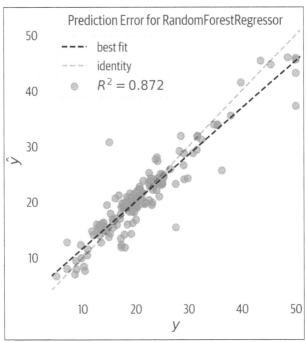

Figure 15-4. Prediction error. Plots predicted y (y-hat) versus actual y.

CHAPTER 16

Explaining Regression Models

Most of the techniques used to explain classification models apply to regression models. In this chapter, I will show how to use the SHAP library to interpret regression models.

We will interpret an XGBoost model for the Boston housing dataset:

```
>>> import xgboost as xgb
>>> xgr = xgb.XGBRegressor(
...     random_state=42, base_score=0.5
... )
>>> xgr.fit(bos_X_train, bos_y_train)
```

Shapley

I'm a big fan of Shapley because it is model agnostic. This library also gives us global insight into our model and helps explain individual predictions. If you have a black-box model, I find it very useful.

We will first look at the prediction for index 5. Our model predicts the value to be 27.26:

```
>>> sample_idx = 5
>>> xgr.predict(bos_X.iloc[[sample_idx]])
array([27.269186], dtype=float32)
```

To use the model, we have to create a `TreeExplainer` from our model and estimate the SHAP values for our samples. If we want to use Jupyter and have an interactive interface, we also need to call the `initjs` function:

```
>>> import shap
>>> shap.initjs()

>>> exp = shap.TreeExplainer(xgr)
>>> vals = exp.shap_values(bos_X)
```

With the explainer and the SHAP values, we can create a force plot to explain the prediction (see Figure 16-1). This informs us that the base prediction is 23, and that the population status (LSTAT) and property tax rate (TAX) push the price up, while the number of rooms (RM) pushes the price down:

```
>>> shap.force_plot(
...       exp.expected_value,
...       vals[sample_idx],
...       bos_X.iloc[sample_idx],
... )
```

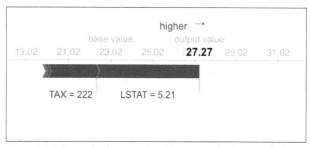

Figure 16-1. Force plot for regression. The expected value is pushed up from 23 to 27 due to the population status and tax rate.

We can view the force plot for all of the samples as well to get an overall feel of the behavior. If we are using the interactive JavaScript mode on Jupyter, we can mouse over the samples and see what features are impacting the result (see Figure 16-2):

```
>>> shap.force_plot(
...     exp.expected_value, vals, bos_X
... )
```

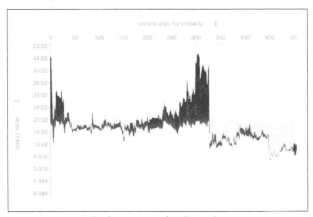

Figure 16-2. Force plot for regression for all samples.

From the force plot of the sample, we saw that the LSTAT feature had a big impact. To visualize how LSTAT affects the result, we can create a dependence plot. The library will automatically choose a feature to color it by (you can provide the `interaction_index` parameter to set your own).

From the dependence plot for LSTAT (see Figure 16-3), we can see that as LSTAT increases (the percent of lower status population), the SHAP value goes down (pushing down the target). A very low LSTAT value pushes SHAP up. From viewing the coloring of the TAX (property tax rate), it appears that as the rate goes down (more blue), the SHAP value goes up:

```
>>> fig, ax = plt.subplots(figsize=(6, 4))
>>> shap.dependence_plot("LSTAT", vals, bos_X)
>>> fig.savefig(
...     "images/mlpr_1603.png",
...     bbox_inches="tight",
...     dpi=300,
... )
```

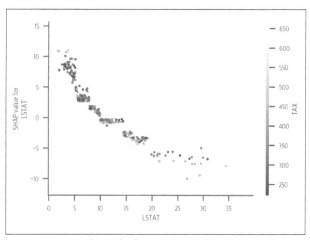

Figure 16-3. Dependence plot for LSTAT. As LSTAT goes up, the predicted value goes down.

Here is another dependence plot, shown in Figure 16-4, to explore the DIS (distance to employment centers). It appears that this feature has little effect unless it is very small:

```
>>> fig, ax = plt.subplots(figsize=(6, 4))
>>> shap.dependence_plot(
...     "DIS", vals, bos_X, interaction_index="RM"
... )
>>> fig.savefig(
...     "images/mlpr_1604.png",
...     bbox_inches="tight",
...     dpi=300,
... )
```

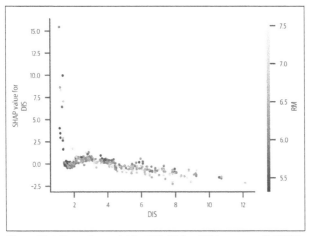

Figure 16-4. Dependence plot for DIS. Unless DIS is very small, SHAP stays relatively flat.

Finally, we will look at the global effect of the features using a summary plot (see Figure 16-5). The features at the top have the most impact to the model. From this view you can see that large values of RM (number of rooms) push up the target a lot, while medium and smaller values push it down a little:

```
>>> fig, ax = plt.subplots(figsize=(6, 4))
>>> shap.summary_plot(vals, bos_X)
>>> fig.savefig(
...     "images/mlpr_1605.png",
...     bbox_inches="tight",
...     dpi=300,
... )
```

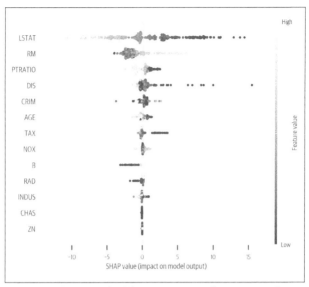

Figure 16-5. Summary plot. The most important features are at the top.

The SHAP library is a great tool to have in your toolbelt. It helps understand the global impact of features and also helps explain individual predictions.

CHAPTER 17

Dimensionality Reduction

There are many techniques to decompose features into a smaller subset. This can be useful for exploratory data analysis, visualization, making predictive models, or clustering.

In this chapter we will explore the Titanic dataset using various techniques. We will look at PCA, UMAP, t-SNE, and PHATE.

Here is the data:

```
>>> ti_df = tweak_titanic(orig_df)
>>> std_cols = "pclass,age,sibsp,fare".split(",")
>>> X_train, X_test, y_train, y_test =
get_train_test_X_y(
...       ti_df, "survived", std_cols=std_cols
... )
>>> X = pd.concat([X_train, X_test])
>>> y = pd.concat([y_train, y_test])
```

PCA

Principal Component Analysis (PCA) takes a matrix (X) of rows (samples) and columns (features). PCA returns a new matrix that has columns that are linear combinations of the original columns. These linear combinations maximize the variance.

Each column is orthogonal (a right angle) to the other columns. The columns are sorted in order of decreasing variance.

Scikit-learn has an implementation of this model. It is best to standardize the data prior to running the algorithm. After calling the .fit method, you will have access to an .explained_variance_ratio_ attribute that lists the percentage of variance in each column.

PCA is useful to visualize data in two (or three) dimensions. It is also used as a preprocessing step to filter out random noise in data. It is good for finding global structures, but not local ones, and works well with linear data.

In this example, we are going to run PCA on the Titanic features. The PCA class is a *transformer* in scikit-learn; you call the .fit method to teach it how to get the principal components, then you call .transform to convert a matrix into a matrix of principal components:

```
>>> from sklearn.decomposition import PCA
>>> from sklearn.preprocessing import (
...     StandardScaler,
... )
>>> pca = PCA(random_state=42)
>>> X_pca = pca.fit_transform(
...     StandardScaler().fit_transform(X)
... )
>>> pca.explained_variance_ratio_
array([0.23917891, 0.21623078, 0.19265028,
  0.10460882, 0.08170342, 0.07229959,
  0.05133752, 0.04199068])

>>> pca.components_[0]
arrayarray([-0.63368693,  0.39682566,
  0.00614498,  0.11488415,  0.58075352,
  -0.19046812, -0.21190808, -0.09631388])
```

Instance parameters:

`n_components=None`
> Number of components to generate. If None, return same number as number of columns. Can be a float (0, 1), then will create as many components as needed to get that ratio of variance.

`copy=True`
> Will mutate data on `.fit` if True.

`whiten=False`
> Whiten data after transform to ensure uncorrelated components.

`svd_solver='auto'`
> `'auto'` runs `'randomized'` SVD if n_components is less than 80% of the smallest dimension (faster, but an approximation). Otherwise runs `'full'`.

`tol=0.0`
> Tolerance for singular values.

`iterated_power='auto'`
> Number of iterations for `'randomized'` svd_solver.

`random_state=None`
> Random state for `'randomized'` svd_solver.

Attributes:

`components_`
> Principal components (columns of linear combination weights for original features).

`explained_variance_`
> Amount of variance for each component.

`explained_variance_ratio_`
> Amount of variance for each component normalized (sums to 1).

`singular_values_`
> Singular values for each component.

`mean_`

    Mean of each feature.

`n_components_`

    When `n_components` is a float, this is the size of the components.

`noise_variance_`

    Estimated noise covariance.

Plotting the cumulative sum of the explained variance ratio is called a *scree plot* (see Figure 17-1). It will show how much information is stored in the components. You can use the *elbow method* to see if it bends to determine how many components to use:

```
>>> fig, ax = plt.subplots(figsize=(6, 4))
>>> ax.plot(pca.explained_variance_ratio_)
>>> ax.set(
...     xlabel="Component",
...     ylabel="Percent of Explained variance",
...     title="Scree Plot",
...     ylim=(0, 1),
... )
>>> fig.savefig(
...     "images/mlpr_1701.png",
...     dpi=300,
...     bbox_inches="tight",
... )
```

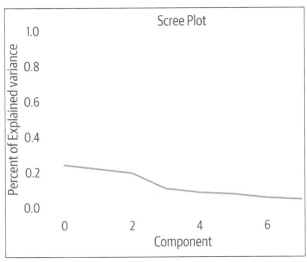

Figure 17-1. PCA scree plot.

Another way to view this data is using a cumulative plot (see Figure 17-2). Our original data had 8 columns, but from the plot it appears that we keep around 90% of the variance if we use just 4 of the PCA components:

```
>>> fig, ax = plt.subplots(figsize=(6, 4))
>>> ax.plot(
...     np.cumsum(pca.explained_variance_ratio_)
... )
>>> ax.set(
...     xlabel="Component",
...     ylabel="Percent of Explained variance",
...     title="Cumulative Variance",
...     ylim=(0, 1),
... )
>>> fig.savefig("images/mlpr_1702.png", dpi=300)
```

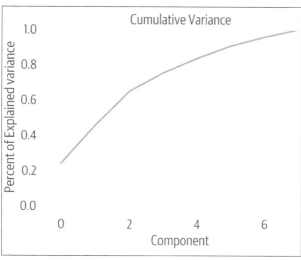

Figure 17-2. PCA cumulative explained variance.

How much do features impact components? Use the matplotlib imshow function to plot the components along the x axis and the original features along the y axis (see Figure 17-3). The darker the color, the more the original column contributes to the component.

It looks like the first component is heavily influenced by the pclass, age, and fare columns. (Using the spectral colormap (cmap) emphasizes nonzero values, and providing vmin and vmax adds limits to the colorbar legend.)

```
>>> fig, ax = plt.subplots(figsize=(6, 4))
>>> plt.imshow(
...     pca.components_.T,
...     cmap="Spectral",
...     vmin=-1,
...     vmax=1,
... )
>>> plt.yticks(range(len(X.columns)), X.columns)
>>> plt.xticks(range(8), range(1, 9))
```

```
>>> plt.xlabel("Principal Component")
>>> plt.ylabel("Contribution")
>>> plt.title(
...     "Contribution of Features to Components"
... )
>>> plt.colorbar()
>>> fig.savefig("images/mlpr_1703.png", dpi=300)
```

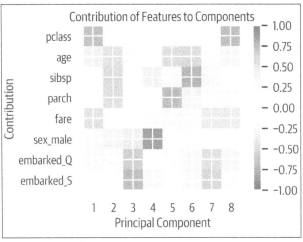

Figure 17-3. PCA features in components.

An alternative view is to look at a bar plot (see Figure 17-4). Each component is shown with the contributions from the original data:

```
>>> fig, ax = plt.subplots(figsize=(8, 4))
>>> pd.DataFrame(
...     pca.components_, columns=X.columns
... ).plot(kind="bar", ax=ax).legend(
...     bbox_to_anchor=(1, 1)
... )
>>> fig.savefig("images/mlpr_1704.png", dpi=300)
```

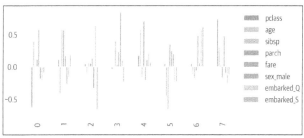

Figure 17-4. PCA features in components.

If we have many features, we may want to limit the plots above by showing only features that meet a minimum weight. Here is code to find all the features in the first two components that have absolute values of at least .5:

```
>>> comps = pd.DataFrame(
...     pca.components_, columns=X.columns
... )
>>> min_val = 0.5
>>> num_components = 2
>>> pca_cols = set()
>>> for i in range(num_components):
...     parts = comps.iloc[i][
...         comps.iloc[i].abs() > min_val
...     ]
...     pca_cols.update(set(parts.index))
>>> pca_cols
{'fare', 'parch', 'pclass', 'sibsp'}
```

PCA is commonly used to visualize high dimension datasets in two components. Here we visualize the Titanic features in 2D. They are colored by survival status. Sometimes clusters may appear in the visualization. In this case, there doesn't appear to be clustering of survivors (see Figure 17-5).

We generate this visualization using Yellowbrick:

```
>>> from yellowbrick.features.pca import (
...     PCADecomposition,
... )
```

```
>>> fig, ax = plt.subplots(figsize=(6, 4))
>>> colors = ["rg"[j] for j in y]
>>> pca_viz = PCADecomposition(color=colors)
>>> pca_viz.fit_transform(X, y)
>>> pca_viz.poof()
>>> fig.savefig("images/mlpr_1705.png", dpi=300)
```

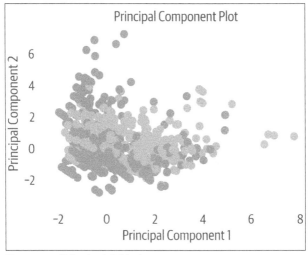

Figure 17-5. Yellowbrick PCA plot.

If you want to color the scatter plot by a column and add a leg-end (not a colorbar), you need to loop over each color and plot that group individually in pandas or matplotlib (or use sea-born). Below we also set the aspect ratio to the ratio of the explained variances for the components we are looking at (see Figure 17-6). Because the second component only has 90% of the first component, it is a little shorter.

Here is the seaborn version:

```
>>> fig, ax = plt.subplots(figsize=(6, 4))
>>> pca_df = pd.DataFrame(
...      X_pca,
...      columns=[
```

```
...            f"PC{i+1}"
...            for i in range(X_pca.shape[1])
...        ],
... )
>>> pca_df["status"] = [
...        ("deceased", "survived")[i] for i in y
... ]
>>> evr = pca.explained_variance_ratio_
>>> ax.set_aspect(evr[1] / evr[0])
>>> sns.scatterplot(
...        x="PC1",
...        y="PC2",
...        hue="status",
...        data=pca_df,
...        alpha=0.5,
...        ax=ax,
... )
>>> fig.savefig(
...        "images/mlpr_1706.png",
...        dpi=300,
...        bbox_inches="tight",
... )
```

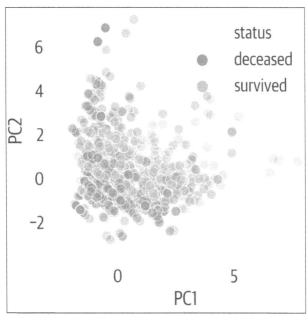

Figure 17-6. Seaborn PCA with legend and relative aspect.

Below, we augment the scatter plot by showing a *loading plot* on top of it. This plot is called a biplot because it has the scatter plot and the loadings (see Figure 17-7). The loadings indicate how strong features are and how they correlate. If their angles are close, they likely correlate. If the angles are at 90 degrees, they likely don't correlate. Finally, if the angle between them is close to 180 degrees, they have a negative correlation:

```
>>> fig, ax = plt.subplots(figsize=(6, 4))
>>> pca_df = pd.DataFrame(
...     X_pca,
...     columns=[
...         f"PC{i+1}"
...         for i in range(X_pca.shape[1])
...     ],
... )
```

```
>>> pca_df["status"] = [
...     ("deceased", "survived")[i] for i in y
... ]
>>> evr = pca.explained_variance_ratio_
>>> x_idx = 0  # x_pc
>>> y_idx = 1  # y_pc
>>> ax.set_aspect(evr[y_idx] / evr[x_idx])
>>> x_col = pca_df.columns[x_idx]
>>> y_col = pca_df.columns[y_idx]
>>> sns.scatterplot(
...     x=x_col,
...     y=y_col,
...     hue="status",
...     data=pca_df,
...     alpha=0.5,
...     ax=ax,
... )
>>> scale = 8
>>> comps = pd.DataFrame(
...     pca.components_, columns=X.columns
... )
>>> for idx, s in comps.T.iterrows():
...     plt.arrow(
...         0,
...         0,
...         s[x_idx] * scale,
...         s[y_idx] * scale,
...         color="k",
...     )
...     plt.text(
...         s[x_idx] * scale,
...         s[y_idx] * scale,
...         idx,
...         weight="bold",
...     )
>>> fig.savefig(
...     "images/mlpr_1707.png",
...     dpi=300,
...     bbox_inches="tight",
... )
```

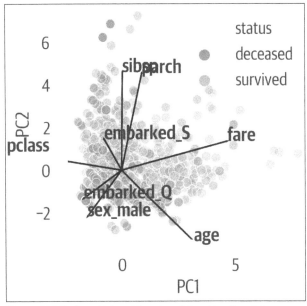

Figure 17-7. Seaborn biplot with scatter plot and loading plot.

From previous tree models, we know that age, fare, and sex are important for determining whether a passenger survived. The first principal component is influenced by pclass, age, and fare, while the fourth is influenced by sex. Let's plot those components against each other.

Again, this plot is scaling the aspect ratio of the plot based on the ratios of variance of the components (see Figure 17-8).

This plot appears to more accurately separate the survivors:

```
>>> fig, ax = plt.subplots(figsize=(6, 4))
>>> pca_df = pd.DataFrame(
...     X_pca,
...     columns=[
...         f"PC{i+1}"
...         for i in range(X_pca.shape[1])
```

```
...     ],
... )
>>> pca_df["status"] = [
...     ("deceased", "survived")[i] for i in y
... ]
>>> evr = pca.explained_variance_ratio_
>>> ax.set_aspect(evr[3] / evr[0])
>>> sns.scatterplot(
...     x="PC1",
...     y="PC4",
...     hue="status",
...     data=pca_df,
...     alpha=0.5,
...     ax=ax,
... )
>>> fig.savefig(
...     "images/mlpr_1708.png",
...     dpi=300,
...     bbox_inches="tight",
... )
```

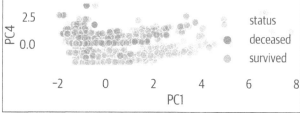

Figure 17-8. PCA plot showing components 1 against 4.

Matplotlib can create pretty plots, but it is less useful for inter-active plots. When performing PCA, it is often useful to view the data for scatter plots. I have included a function that uses the Bokeh library (*https://bokeh.pydata.org*) for interacting with scatter plots (see Figure 17-9). It works well in Jupyter:

```
>>> from bokeh.io import output_notebook
>>> from bokeh import models, palettes, transform
>>> from bokeh.plotting import figure, show
```

```
>>>
>>> def bokeh_scatter(
...     x,
...     y,
...     data,
...     hue=None,
...     label_cols=None,
...     size=None,
...     legend=None,
...     alpha=0.5,
... ):
...     """
...     x - x column name to plot
...     y - y column name to plot
...     data - pandas DataFrame
...     hue - column name to color by (numeric)
...     legend - column name to label by
...     label_cols - columns to use in tooltip
...                 (None all in DataFrame)
...     size - size of points in screen space unigs
...     alpha - transparency
...     """
...     output_notebook()
...     circle_kwargs = {}
...     if legend:
...         circle_kwargs["legend"] = legend
...     if size:
...         circle_kwargs["size"] = size
...     if hue:
...         color_seq = data[hue]
...         mapper = models.LinearColorMapper(
...             palette=palettes.viridis(256),
...             low=min(color_seq),
...             high=max(color_seq),
...         )
...         circle_kwargs[
...             "fill_color"
...         ] = transform.transform(hue, mapper)
...     ds = models.ColumnDataSource(data)
...     if label_cols is None:
```

```
...                label_cols = data.columns
...          tool_tips = sorted(
...              [
...                  (x, "@{}".format(x))
...                  for x in label_cols
...              ],
...              key=lambda tup: tup[0],
...          )
...          hover = models.HoverTool(
...              tooltips=tool_tips
...          )
...          fig = figure(
...              tools=[
...                  hover,
...                  "pan",
...                  "zoom_in",
...                  "zoom_out",
...                  "reset",
...              ],
...              toolbar_location="below",
...          )
...
...          fig.circle(
...              x,
...              y,
...              source=ds,
...              alpha=alpha,
...              **circle_kwargs
...          )
...          show(fig)
...          return fig
>>> res = bokeh_scatter(
...      "PC1",
...      "PC2",
...      data=pca_df.assign(
...          surv=y.reset_index(drop=True)
...      ),
...      hue="surv",
...      size=10,
```

```
...        legend="surv",
... )
```

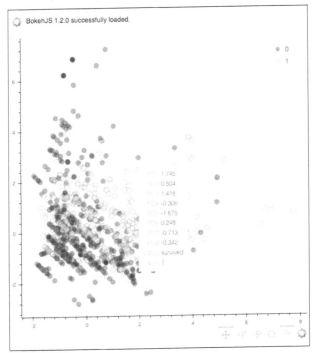

Figure 17-9. Bokeh scatter plot with tooltips.

Yellowbrick can also plot in three dimensions (see Figure 17-10):

```
>>> from yellowbrick.features.pca import (
...        PCADecomposition,
... )
>>> colors = ["rg"[j] for j in y]
>>> pca3_viz = PCADecomposition(
...        proj_dim=3, color=colors
... )
>>> pca3_viz.fit_transform(X, y)
```

```
>>> pca3_viz.finalize()
>>> fig = plt.gcf()
>>> plt.tight_layout()
>>> fig.savefig(
...     "images/mlpr_1710.png",
...     dpi=300,
...     bbox_inches="tight",
... )
```

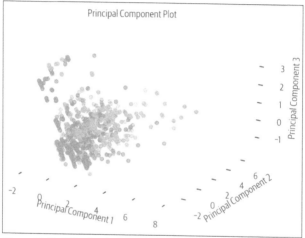

Figure 17-10. Yellowbrick 3D PCA.

The scprep library (*https://oreil.ly/Jdq1s*) (which is a dependency for the PHATE library, which we discuss shortly) has a useful plotting function. The rotate_scatter3d function can generate a plot that will animate in Jupyter (see Figure 17-11). This makes it easier to understand 3D plots.

You can use this library to visualize any 3D data, not just PHATE:

```
>>> import scprep
>>> scprep.plot.rotate_scatter3d(
...     X_pca[:, :3],
...     c=y,
```

```
...        cmap="Spectral",
...        figsize=(8, 6),
...        label_prefix="Principal Component",
... )
```

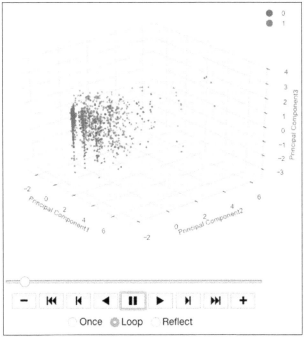

Figure 17-11. scprep 3D PCA animation.

If you change the matplotlib cell magic mode in Jupyter to note
book, you can get an interactive 3D plot from matplotlib (see
Figure 17-12).

```
>>> from mpl_toolkits.mplot3d import Axes3D
>>> fig = plt.figure(figsize=(6, 4))
>>> ax = fig.add_subplot(111, projection="3d")
>>> ax.scatter(
...     xs=X_pca[:, 0],
...     ys=X_pca[:, 1],
```

```
...       zs=X_pca[:, 2],
...       c=y,
...       cmap="viridis",
... )
>>> ax.set_xlabel("PC 1")
>>> ax.set_ylabel("PC 2")
>>> ax.set_zlabel("PC 3")
```

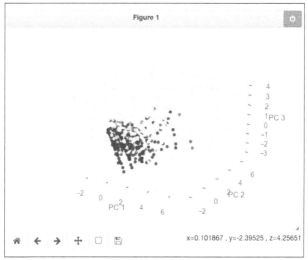

Figure 17-12. Matplotlib interactive 3D PCA with notebook mode.

WARNING

Note that switching the cell magic for matplotlib in Jupyter from:

```
% matplotlib inline
```

to:

```
% matplotlib notebook
```

can sometimes cause Jupyter to stop responding. Tread with caution.

UMAP

Uniform Manifold Approximation and Projection (UMAP) (*https://oreil.ly/qF8RJ*) is a dimensionality reduction technique that uses manifold learning. As such it tends to keeps similar items together topologically. It tries to preserve both the global and the local structure, as opposed to t-SNE (explained in "t-SNE" on page 264), which favors local structure.

The Python implementation doesn't have multicore support.

Normalization of features is a good idea to get values on the same scale.

UMAP is very sensitive to hyperparameters (n_neighbors, min_dist, n_components, or metric). Here are some examples:

```
>>> import umap
>>> u = umap.UMAP(random_state=42)
>>> X_umap = u.fit_transform(
...      StandardScaler().fit_transform(X)
... )
>>> X_umap.shape
(1309, 2)
```

Instance parameters:

n_neighbors=15
> Local neighborhood size. Larger means use a global view, smaller means more local.

n_components=2
> Number of dimensions for embedding.

metric='euclidean'
> Metric to use for distance. Can be a function that accepts two 1D arrays and returns a float.

n_epochs=None
> Number of training epochs. Default will be 200 or 500 (depending on size of data).

```
learning_rate=1.0
```
    Learning rate for embedding optimization.

```
init='spectral'
```
    Initialization type. Spectral embedding is the default. Can
    be `'random'` or a numpy array of locations.

```
min_dist=0.1
```
    Between 0 and 1. Minimum distance between embedded
    points. Smaller means more clumps, larger means spread
    out.

```
spread=1.0
```
    Determines distance of embedded points.

```
set_op_mix_ratio=1.0
```
    Between 0 and 1: fuzzy union (1) or fuzzy intersection (0).

```
local_connectivity=1.0
```
    Number of neighbors for local connectivity. As this goes
    up, more local connections are created.

```
repulsion_strength=1.0
```
    Repulsion strength. Higher values give more weight to
    negative samples.

```
negative_sample_rate=5
```
    Negative samples per positive sample. Higher value has
    more repulsion, more optimization costs, and better
    accuracy.

```
transform_queue_size=4.0
```
    Aggressiveness for nearest neighbors search. Higher value
    is lower performance but better accuracy.

```
a=None
```
    Parameter to control embedding. If equal to `None`, UMAP
    determines these from `min_dist` and `spread`.

```
b=None
```
    Parameter to control embedding. If equal to `None`, UMAP
    determines these from `min_dist` and `spread`.

`random_state=None`
> Random seed.

`metric_kwds=None`
> Metrics dictionary for additional parameters if function is used for `metric`. Also `minkowsi` (and other metrics) can be parameterized with this.

`angular_rp_forest=False`
> Use angular random projection.

`target_n_neighbors=-1`
> Number of neighbors for simplicity set.

`target_metric='categorical'`
> For using supervised reduction. Can also be `'L1'` or `'L2'`. Also supports a function that takes two arrays from X as input and returns the distance value between them.

`target_metric_kwds=None`
> Metrics dictionary to use if function is used for `target_metric`.

`target_weight=0.5`
> Weighting factor. Between 0.0 and 1.0, where 0 means base on data only, and 1 means base on target only.

`transform_seed=42`
> Random seed for transform operations.

`verbose=False`
> Verbosity.

Attributes:

`embedding_`
> The embedding results

Let's visualize the default results of UMAP on the Titanic dataset (see Figure 17-13):

```
>>> fig, ax = plt.subplots(figsize=(8, 4))
>>> pd.DataFrame(X_umap).plot(
...     kind="scatter",
```

```
...        x=0,
...        y=1,
...        ax=ax,
...        c=y,
...        alpha=0.2,
...        cmap="Spectral",
... )
>>> fig.savefig("images/mlpr_1713.png", dpi=300)
```

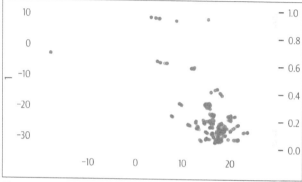

Figure 17-13. UMAP results.

To adjust the results of UMAP, focus on the n_neighbors and min_dist hyperparameters first. Here are illustrations of changing those values (see Figures 17-14 and 17-15):

```
>>> X_std = StandardScaler().fit_transform(X)
>>> fig, axes = plt.subplots(2, 2, figsize=(6, 4))
>>> axes = axes.reshape(4)
>>> for i, n in enumerate([2, 5, 10, 50]):
...        ax = axes[i]
...        u = umap.UMAP(
...            random_state=42, n_neighbors=n
...        )
...        X_umap = u.fit_transform(X_std)
...
...        pd.DataFrame(X_umap).plot(
...            kind="scatter",
...            x=0,
```

```
...             y=1,
...             ax=ax,
...             c=y,
...             cmap="Spectral",
...             alpha=0.5,
...         )
...     ax.set_title(f"nn={n}")
>>> plt.tight_layout()
>>> fig.savefig("images/mlpr_1714.png", dpi=300)
```

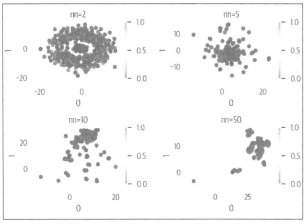

Figure 17-14. UMAP results adjusting n_neighbors.

```
>>> fig, axes = plt.subplots(2, 2, figsize=(6, 4))
>>> axes = axes.reshape(4)
>>> for i, n in enumerate([0, 0.33, 0.66, 0.99]):
...     ax = axes[i]
...     u = umap.UMAP(random_state=42, min_dist=n)
...     X_umap = u.fit_transform(X_std)
...     pd.DataFrame(X_umap).plot(
...         kind="scatter",
...         x=0,
...         y=1,
...         ax=ax,
...         c=y,
...         cmap="Spectral",
```

```
...         alpha=0.5,
...     )
...     ax.set_title(f"min_dist={n}")
>>> plt.tight_layout()
>>> fig.savefig("images/mlpr_1715.png", dpi=300)
```

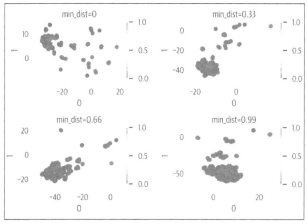

Figure 17-15. UMAP results adjusting min_dist.

Sometimes PCA is performed before UMAP to reduce the dimensions and speed up the computations.

t-SNE

The t-Distributed Stochastic Neighboring Embedding (t-SNE) technique is a visualization and dimensionality reduction technique. It uses distributions of the input and low dimension embedding, and minimizes the joint probabilities between them. Because this is computationally intensive, you might not be able to use this technique with a large dataset.

One characteristic of t-SNE is that it is quite sensitive to hyperparameters. Also, while it preserves local clusters quite well, global information is not preserved. As such, the distance between clusters is meaningless. Finally, this is not a deterministic algorithm and may not converge.

It is a good idea to standardize the data before using this technique:

```
>>> from sklearn.manifold import TSNE
>>> X_std = StandardScaler().fit_transform(X)
>>> ts = TSNE()
>>> X_tsne = ts.fit_transform(X_std)
```

Instance parameters:

n_components=2
> Number of dimensions for embedding.

perplexity=30.0
> Suggested values are between 5 and 50. Smaller numbers tend to make tighter clumps.

early_exaggeration=12.0
> Controls cluster tightness and spacing between them. Larger values mean larger spacing.

learning_rate=200.0
> Usually between 10 and 1000. If data looks like a ball, lower it. If data looks compressed, raise it.

n_iter=1000
> Number of iterations.

n_iter_without_progress=300
> Abort if no progress after this number of iterations.

min_grad_norm=1e-07
> Optimization stops if the gradient norm is below this value.

metric='euclidean'
> Distance metric from scipy.spatial.distance.pdist, pairwise.PAIRWISE_DISTANCE_METRIC, or a function.

init='random'
> Embedding initialization.

```
verbose=0
```
Verbosity.

```
random_state=None
```
Random seed.

```
method='barnes_hut'
```
Gradient calculation algorithm.

```
angle=0.5
```
For gradient calculation. Less than .2 increases runtime. Greater than .8 increases error.

Attributes:

```
embedding_
```
Embedding vectors

```
kl_divergence_
```
Kullback-Leibler divergence

```
n_iter_
```
Number of iterations

Here's a visualization of the results of t-SNE using matplotlib (see Figure 17-16):

```
>>> fig, ax = plt.subplots(figsize=(6, 4))
>>> colors = ["rg"[j] for j in y]
>>> scat = ax.scatter(
...     X_tsne[:, 0],
...     X_tsne[:, 1],
...     c=colors,
...     alpha=0.5,
... )
>>> ax.set_xlabel("Embedding 1")
>>> ax.set_ylabel("Embedding 2")
>>> fig.savefig("images/mlpr_1716.png", dpi=300)
```

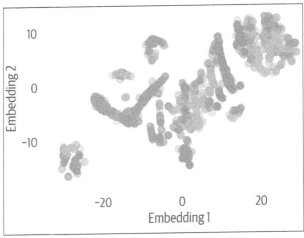

Figure 17-16. t-SNE result with matplotlib.

Changing the value of `perplexity` can have big effects on the plot (see Figure 17-17). Here are a few different values:

```
>>> fig, axes = plt.subplots(2, 2, figsize=(6, 4))
>>> axes = axes.reshape(4)
>>> for i, n in enumerate((2, 30, 50, 100)):
...     ax = axes[i]
...     t = TSNE(random_state=42, perplexity=n)
...     X_tsne = t.fit_transform(X)
...     pd.DataFrame(X_tsne).plot(
...         kind="scatter",
...         x=0,
...         y=1,
...         ax=ax,
...         c=y,
...         cmap="Spectral",
...         alpha=0.5,
...     )
...     ax.set_title(f"perplexity={n}")
... plt.tight_layout()
... fig.savefig("images/mlpr_1717.png", dpi=300)
```

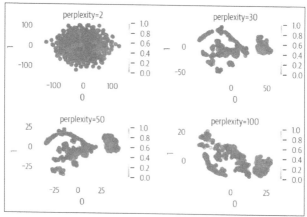

Figure 17-17. Changing `perplexity` for t-SNE.

PHATE

Potential of Heat-diffusion for Affinity-based Trajectory Embedding (PHATE (*https://phate.readthedocs.io*)) is a tool for visualization of high dimensional data. It tends to keep both global structure (like PCA) and local structure (like t-SNE).

PHATE first encodes local information (points close to each other should remain close). It uses "diffusion" to discover global data, then reduce dimensionality:

```
>>> import phate
>>> p = phate.PHATE(random_state=42)
>>> X_phate = p.fit_transform(X)
>>> X_phate.shape
```

Instance parameters:

`n_components=2`
> Number of dimensions.

`knn=5`
> Number of neighbors for the kernel. Increase if the embedding is disconnected or dataset is larger than 100,000 samples.

`decay=40`
> Decay rate of kernel. Lowering this value increases graph connectivity.

`n_landmark=2000`
> Landmarks to use.

`t='auto'`
> Diffusion power. Smoothing is performed on the data. Increase if embedding lacks structure. Decrease if structure is tight and compact.

`gamma=1`
> Log potential (between -1 and 1). If embeddings are concentrated around a single point, try setting this to 0.

`n_pca=100`
> Number of principle components for neighborhood calculation.

`knn_dist='euclidean'`
> KNN metric.

`mds_dist='euclidean'`
> Multidimensional scaling (MDS) metric.

`mds='metric'`
> MDS algorithm for dimension reduction.

`n_jobs=1`
> Number of CPUs to use.

`random_state=None`
> Random seed.

```
verbose=1
```
Verbosity.

Attributes (note that these aren't followed by _):

```
X
```
Input data

```
embedding
```
Embedding space

```
diff_op
```
Diffusion operator

```
graph
```
KNN graph built from input

Here is an example of using PHATE (see Figure 17-18):

```
>>> fig, ax = plt.subplots(figsize=(6, 4))
>>> phate.plot.scatter2d(p, c=y, ax=ax, alpha=0.5)
>>> fig.savefig("images/mlpr_1718.png", dpi=300)
```

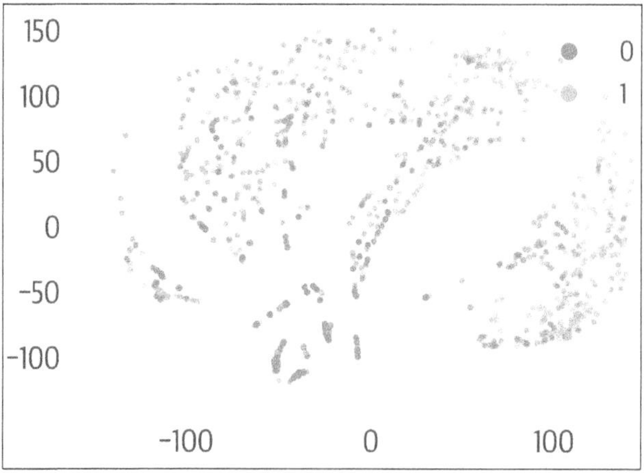

Figure 17-18. PHATE results.

As noted in the instance parameters above, there are a few parameters that we can adjust to change the behavior of the model. Below is an example of adjusting the knn parameter (see Figure 17-19). Note that if we use the .set_params method, it will speed up the calculation as it uses the precomputed graph and diffusion operator:

```
>>> fig, axes = plt.subplots(2, 2, figsize=(6, 4))
>>> axes = axes.reshape(4)
>>> p = phate.PHATE(random_state=42, n_jobs=-1)

>>> for i, n in enumerate((2, 5, 20, 100)):
...     ax = axes[i]
...     p.set_params(knn=n)
...     X_phate = p.fit_transform(X)
...     pd.DataFrame(X_phate).plot(
...         kind="scatter",
...         x=0,
...         y=1,
...         ax=ax,
...         c=y,
...         cmap="Spectral",
...         alpha=0.5,
...     )
...     ax.set_title(f"knn={n}")
... plt.tight_layout()
... fig.savefig("images/mlpr_1719.png", dpi=300)
```

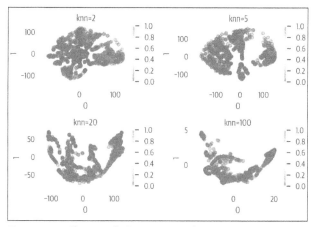

Figure 17-19. Changing the knn parameter for PHATE.

CHAPTER 18

Clustering

Clustering is an unsupervised machine learning technique used to divide a group into cohorts. It is unsupervised because we don't give the model any labels; it just inspects the features and determines which samples are similar and belong in a cluster. In this chapter, we will look at the K-means and hierarchical clustering methods. We will also explore the Titanic dataset again using various techniques.

K-Means

The K-means algorithm requires the user to pick the number of clusters or "k." It then randomly chooses k centroids and assigns each sample to a cluster based on a distance metric from the centroid. Following the assignment, it recalculates the centroids based on the center of every sample assigned to a label. It then repeats assigning samples to clusters based on the new centroids. After a few iterations it should converge.

Because clustering uses distance metrics to determine which samples are similar, the behavior may change depending on the scale of the data. You can standardize the data and put all of the features on the same scale. Some have suggested that a SME might advise against standardizing if the scale hints that some features have more importance. We will standardize the data here in this example.

In this example, we will cluster the Titanic passengers. We will start with two clusters to see if the clustering can tease apart survival (we won't leak the survival data into the clustering and will only use X, not y).

Unsupervised algorithms have a .fit method and a .predict method. We only pass X into .fit:

```
>>> from sklearn.cluster import KMeans
>>> X_std = preprocessing.Stand
ardScaler().fit_transform(
...     X
... )
>>> km = KMeans(2, random_state=42)
>>> km.fit(X_std)
KMeans(algorithm='auto', copy_x=True,
  init='k-means', max_iter=300,
  n_clusters=2, n_init=10, n_jobs=1,
  precompute_distances='auto',
  random_state=42, tol=0.0001, verbose=0)
```

After the model is trained, we can call the .predict method to assign new samples to a cluster:

```
>>> X_km = km.predict(X)
>>> X_km
array([1, 1, 1, ..., 1, 1, 1], dtype=int32)
```

Instance parameters:

n_clusters=8
    Number of clusters to create.

init='kmeans++'
    Initialization method.

n_init=10
    Number of times to run the algorithm with different centroids. Best score will win.

`max_iter=300`
    Number of iterations for a run.

`tol=0.0001`
    Tolerance until convergence.

`precompute_distances='auto'`
    Precompute distances (takes more memory but is faster). `auto` will precompute if n_samples * n_clusters is less than or equal to 12 million.

`verbose=0`
    Verbosity.

`random_state=None`
    Random seed.

`copy_x=True`
    Copy data before computing.

`n_jobs=1`
    Number of CPUs to use.

`algorithm='auto'`
    K-means algorithm. `'full'` works with sparse data, but `'elkan'` is more efficient. `'auto'` uses `'elkan'` with dense data.

Attributes:

`cluster_centers_`
    Coordinates of centers

`labels_`
    Labels for samples

`inertia_`
    Sum of squared distance to cluster centroid

`n_iter_`
    Number of iterations

If you don't know ahead of time how many clusters you need, you can run the algorithm with a range of sizes and evaluate various metrics. It can be tricky.

You can roll your own elbow plot using the `.inertia_` calculation. Look for where the curve bends as that is potentially a good choice for the number of clusters. In this case, the curve is smooth, but after eight there doesn't seem to be much improvement (see Figure 18-1).

For plots without an elbow, we have a few options. We can use other metrics, some of which are shown below. We can also inspect a visualization of the clustering and see if clusters are visible. We can add features to the data and see if that helps with clustering.

Here is the code for an elbow plot:

```
>>> inertias = []
>>> sizes = range(2, 12)
>>> for k in sizes:
...     k2 = KMeans(random_state=42, n_clusters=k)
...     k2.fit(X)
...     inertias.append(k2.inertia_)
>>> fig, ax = plt.subplots(figsize=(6, 4))
>>> pd.Series(inertias, index=sizes).plot(ax=ax)
>>> ax.set_xlabel("K")
>>> ax.set_ylabel("Inertia")
>>> fig.savefig("images/mlpr_1801.png", dpi=300)
```

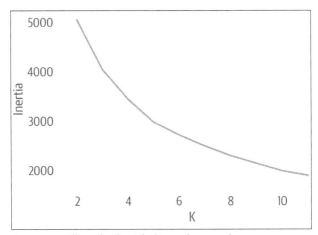

Figure 18-1. Elbow plot that is looking rather smooth.

Scikit-learn has other clustering metrics when the ground truth labels are not known. We can calculate and plot those as well. The *Silhouette Coefficient* is a value between -1 and 1. The higher the score, the better. 1 indicates tight clusters, and 0 means overlapping clusters. From that measure, two clusters gives us the best score.

The *Calinski-Harabasz Index* is the ratio of between-cluster dispersion and within-cluster dispersion. A higher score is better. Two clusters gives the best score for this metric.

The *Davis-Bouldin Index* is the average similarity between each cluster and the closest cluster. Scores range from 0 and up. 0 indicates better clustering.

Here we will plot inertia, the silhouette coefficient, the Calinski-Harabasz Index, and the Davies-Bouldin Index over a range of cluster sizes to see if there is a clear size of clusters for the data (see Figure 18-2). It appears that most of these metrics agree on two clusters:

```
>>> from sklearn import metrics
>>> inertias = []
```

```
>>> sils = []
>>> chs = []
>>> dbs = []
>>> sizes = range(2, 12)
>>> for k in sizes:
...     k2 = KMeans(random_state=42, n_clusters=k)
...     k2.fit(X_std)
...     inertias.append(k2.inertia_)
...     sils.append(
...         metrics.silhouette_score(X, k2.labels_)
...     )
...     chs.append(
...         metrics.calinski_harabasz_score(
...             X, k2.labels_
...         )
...     )
...     dbs.append(
...         metrics.davies_bouldin_score(
...             X, k2.labels_
...         )
...     )
>>> fig, ax = plt.subplots(figsize=(6, 4))
>>> (
...     pd.DataFrame(
...         {
...             "inertia": inertias,
...             "silhouette": sils,
...             "calinski": chs,
...             "davis": dbs,
...             "k": sizes,
...         }
...     )
...     .set_index("k")
...     .plot(ax=ax, subplots=True, layout=(2, 2))
... )
>>> fig.savefig("images/mlpr_1802.png", dpi=300)
```

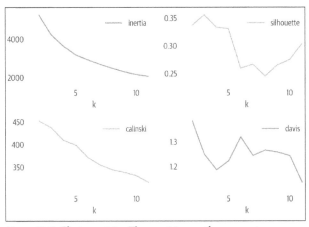

Figure 18-2. Cluster metrics. These metrics mostly agree on two clusters.

Another technique for determining clusters is to visualize the silhouette scores for each cluster. Yellowbrick has a visualizer for this (see Figure 18-3).

The vertical dotted red line in this plot is the average score. One way to interpret it is to make sure that each cluster bumps out above the average, and the cluster scores look decent. Make sure you are using the same x limits (ax.set_xlim). I would choose two clusters from these plots:

```
>>> from yellowbrick.cluster.silhouette import (
...     SilhouetteVisualizer,
... )
>>> fig, axes = plt.subplots(2, 2, figsize=(12, 8))
>>> axes = axes.reshape(4)
>>> for i, k in enumerate(range(2, 6)):
...     ax = axes[i]
...     sil = SilhouetteVisualizer(
...         KMeans(n_clusters=k, random_state=42),
...         ax=ax,
...     )
...     sil.fit(X_std)
```

```
...        sil.finalize()
...        ax.set_xlim(-0.2, 0.8)
>>> plt.tight_layout()
>>> fig.savefig("images/mlpr_1803.png", dpi=300)
```

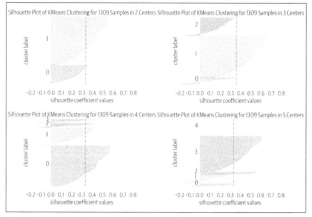

Figure 18-3. Yellowbrick silhouette visualizer

Agglomerative (Hierarchical) Clustering

Agglomerative clustering is another methodology. You start off with each sample in its own cluster. Then you combine the "nearest" clusters. Repeat until done while keeping track of the nearest sizes.

When you have finished this, you will have a *dendrogram*, or a tree that tracks when clusters were created and what the distance metric was. You can use the scipy library to visualize the dendrogram.

We can use scipy to create a dendrogram (see Figure 18-4). As you can see, if you have many samples the leaf nodes are hard to read:

```
>>> from scipy.cluster import hierarchy
>>> fig, ax = plt.subplots(figsize=(6, 4))
>>> dend = hierarchy.dendrogram(
```

```
...        hierarchy.linkage(X_std, method="ward")
... )
>>> fig.savefig("images/mlpr_1804.png", dpi=300)
```

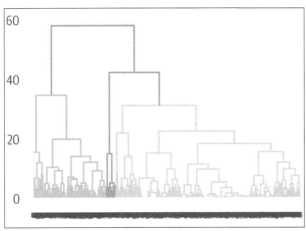

Figure 18-4. Scipy hierarchical clustering dendrogram

Once you have the dendrogram, you have all the clusters (from one to the size of the samples). The heights represent how similar clusters are when they are joined. In order to find how many clusters are in the data, you would want to "cut" a horizontal line through where it would cross the tallest lines.

In this case, it looks like when you perform that cut, you have three clusters.

The previous plot was a little noisy with all of the samples in it. You can also use the `truncate_mode` parameter to combine the leaves into a single node (see Figure 18-5):

```
>>> from scipy.cluster import hierarchy
>>> fig, ax = plt.subplots(figsize=(6, 4))
>>> dend = hierarchy.dendrogram(
...        hierarchy.linkage(X_std, method="ward"),
...        truncate_mode="lastp",
...        p=20,
```

```
...         show_contracted=True,
...     )
>>> fig.savefig("images/mlpr_1805.png", dpi=300)
```

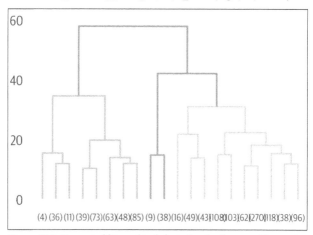

Figure 18-5. Truncated hierarchical clustering dendrogram. If we cut across the largest vertical lines, we get three clusters.

Once we know how many clusters we need, we can use scikit-learn to create a model:

```
>>> from sklearn.cluster import (
...     AgglomerativeClustering,
... )
>>> ag = AgglomerativeClustering(
...     n_clusters=4,
...     affinity="euclidean",
...     linkage="ward",
... )
>>> ag.fit(X)
```

The fastcluster package (*https://oreil.ly/OuNuo*) provides an optimized agglomerative clustering package if the scikit-learn implementation is too slow.

Understanding Clusters

Using K-means on the Titanic dataset, we will make two clusters. We can use the grouping functionality in pandas to examine the differences in the clusters. The code below examines the mean and variance for each feature. It appears that the mean value for pclass varies quite a bit.

I'm sticking the survival data back in to see if the clustering was related to that:

```
>>> km = KMeans(n_clusters=2)
>>> km.fit(X_std)
>>> labels = km.predict(X_std)
>>> (
...      X.assign(cluster=labels, survived=y)
...      .groupby("cluster")
...      .agg(["mean", "var"])
...      .T
... )
cluster                    0         1
pclass     mean   0.526538 -1.423831
           var    0.266089  0.136175
age        mean  -0.280471  0.921668
           var    0.653027  1.145303
sibsp      mean  -0.010464 -0.107849
           var    1.163848  0.303881
parch      mean   0.387540  0.378453
           var    0.829570  0.540587
fare       mean  -0.349335  0.886400
           var    0.056321  2.225399
sex_male   mean   0.678986  0.552486
           var    0.218194  0.247930
```

```
embarked_Q  mean    0.123548    0.016575
            var     0.108398    0.016345
embarked_S  mean    0.741288    0.585635
            var     0.191983    0.243339
survived    mean    0.596685    0.299894
            var     0.241319    0.210180
```

NOTE

In Jupyter you can tack on the following code to a Data-
Frame, and it will highlight the high and low values of each
row. This is useful for visually seeing which values stand
out in the above cluster summary:

```
.style.background_gradient(cmap='RdBu',
axis=1)
```

In Figure 18-6 we plot a bar plot of the means for each cluster:

```
>>> fig, ax = plt.subplots(figsize=(6, 4))
... (
...       X.assign(cluster=labels, survived=y)
...       .groupby("cluster")
...       .mean()
...       .T.plot.bar(ax=ax)
... )
>>> fig.savefig(
...       "images/mlpr_1806.png",
...       dpi=300,
...       bbox_inches="tight",
... )
```

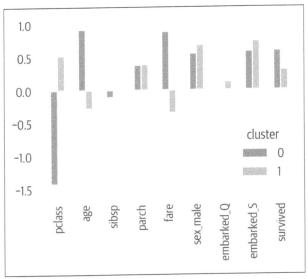

Figure 18-6. Mean values of each cluster

I also like to plot the PCA components, but colored by the cluster label (see Figure 18-7). Here we use Seaborn to do that. It is also interesting to change the values for hue to dive into the features that are distinct for the clusters.

```
>>> fig, ax = plt.subplots(figsize=(6, 4))
>>> sns.scatterplot(
...     "PC1",
...     "PC2",
...     data=X.assign(
...         PC1=X_pca[:, 0],
...         PC2=X_pca[:, 1],
...         cluster=labels,
...     ),
...     hue="cluster",
...     alpha=0.5,
...     ax=ax,
... )
>>> fig.savefig(
```

```
...        "images/mlpr_1807.png",
...        dpi=300,
...        bbox_inches="tight",
... )
```

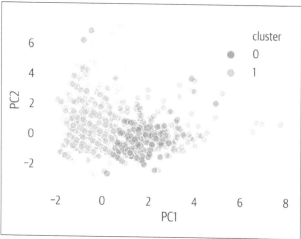

Figure 18-7. PCA plot of clusters

If we want to examine a single feature, we can use the pandas `.describe` method:

```
>>> (
...        X.assign(cluster=label)
...        .groupby("cluster")
...        .age.describe()
...        .T
... )
cluster           0           1
count    362.000000  947.000000
mean       0.921668   -0.280471
std        1.070188    0.808101
min       -2.160126   -2.218578
25%        0.184415   -0.672870
50%        0.867467   -0.283195
```

| 75% | 1.665179 | 0.106480 |
| max | 4.003228 | 3.535618 |

We can also create a surrogate model to explain the clusters. Here we use a decision tree to explain them. This also shows that pclass (which had a large difference in the mean) is very important:

```
>>> dt = tree.DecisionTreeClassifier()
>>> dt.fit(X, labels)
>>> for col, val in sorted(
...     zip(X.columns, dt.feature_importances_),
...     key=lambda col_val: col_val[1],
...     reverse=True,
... ):
...     print(f"{col:10}{val:10.3f}")
pclass        0.902
age           0.074
sex_male      0.016
embarked_S    0.003
fare          0.003
parch         0.003
sibsp         0.000
embarked_Q    0.000
```

And we can visualize the decisions in Figure 18-8. It shows that pclass is the first feature the surrogate looks at to make a decision:

```
>>> dot_data = StringIO()
>>> tree.export_graphviz(
...     dt,
...     out_file=dot_data,
...     feature_names=X.columns,
...     class_names=["0", "1"],
...     max_depth=2,
...     filled=True,
... )
>>> g = pydotplus.graph_from_dot_data(
...     dot_data.getvalue()
... )
>>> g.write_png("images/mlpr_1808.png")
```

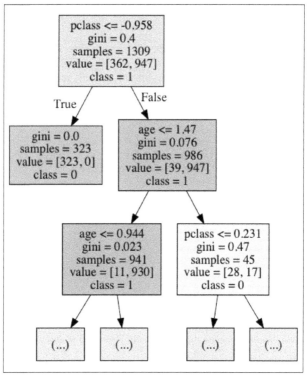

Figure 18-8. Decision tree explaining the clustering

CHAPTER 19

Pipelines

Scikit-learn uses the notion of a pipeline. Using the Pipeline class, you can chain together transformers and models, and treat the whole process like a scikit-learn model. You can even insert custom logic.

Classification Pipeline

Here is an example using the tweak_titanic function inside of a pipeline:

```
>>> from sklearn.base import (
...     BaseEstimator,
...     TransformerMixin,
... )
>>> from sklearn.pipeline import Pipeline

>>> def tweak_titanic(df):
...     df = df.drop(
...         columns=[
...             "name",
...             "ticket",
...             "home.dest",
...             "boat",
...             "body",
...             "cabin",
```

```
...             ]
...         ).pipe(pd.get_dummies, drop_first=True)
...         return df

>>> class TitanicTransformer(
...         BaseEstimator, TransformerMixin
... ):
...         def transform(self, X):
...             # assumes X is output
...             # from reading Excel file
...             X = tweak_titanic(X)
...             X = X.drop(column="survived")
...             return X
...
...         def fit(self, X, y):
...             return self

>>> pipe = Pipeline(
...     [
...         ("titan", TitanicTransformer()),
...         ("impute", impute.IterativeImputer()),
...         (
...             "std",
...             preprocessing.StandardScaler(),
...         ),
...         ("rf", RandomForestClassifier()),
...     ]
... )
```

With a pipeline in hand, we can call .fit and .score on it:

```
>>> from sklearn.model_selection import (
...     train_test_split,
... )
>>> X_train2, X_test2, y_train2, y_test2 =
train_test_split(
...     orig_df,
...     orig_df.survived,
...     test_size=0.3,
...     random_state=42,
... )
```

```
>>> pipe.fit(X_train2, y_train2)
>>> pipe.score(X_test2, y_test2)
0.7913486005089059
```

Pipelines can be used in grid search. Our `param_grid` needs to have the parameters prefixed by the name of the pipe stage, followed by two underscores. In the example below, we add some parameters for the random forest stage:

```
>>> params = {
...     "rf__max_features": [0.4, "auto"],
...     "rf__n_estimators": [15, 200],
... }

>>> grid = model_selection.GridSearchCV(
...     pipe, cv=3, param_grid=params
... )
>>> grid.fit(orig_df, orig_df.survived)
```

Now we can pull out the best parameters and train the final model. (In this case the random forest doesn't improve after grid search.)

```
>>> grid.best_params_
{'rf__max_features': 0.4, 'rf__n_estimators': 15}
>>> pipe.set_params(**grid.best_params_)
>>> pipe.fit(X_train2, y_train2)
>>> pipe.score(X_test2, y_test2)
0.7913486005089059
```

We can use the pipeline where we use scikit-learn models:

```
>>> metrics.roc_auc_score(
...     y_test2, pipe.predict(X_test2)
... )
0.7813688715131023
```

Regression Pipeline

Here is an example of a pipeline that performs linear regression on the Boston dataset:

```
>>> from sklearn.pipeline import Pipeline

>>> reg_pipe = Pipeline(
...     [
...         (
...             "std",
...             preprocessing.StandardScaler(),
...         ),
...         ("lr", LinearRegression()),
...     ]
... )
>>> reg_pipe.fit(bos_X_train, bos_y_train)
>>> reg_pipe.score(bos_X_test, bos_y_test)
0.7112260057484934
```

If we want to pull parts out of the pipeline to examine their properties, we can do that with the .named_steps attribute:

```
>>> reg_pipe.named_steps["lr"].intercept_
23.01581920903956
>>> reg_pipe.named_steps["lr"].coef_
array([-1.10834602,  0.80843998,  0.34313466,
        0.81386426, -1.79804295,  2.913858  ,
       -0.29893918, -2.94251148,  2.09419303,
       -1.44706731, -2.05232232,  1.02375187,
       -3.88579002])_
```

We can use the pipeline in metric calculations as well:

```
>>> from sklearn import metrics
>>> metrics.mean_squared_error(
...     bos_y_test, reg_pipe.predict(bos_X_test)
... )
21.517444231177205
```

PCA Pipeline

Scikit-learn pipelines can also be used for PCA.

Here we standardize the Titanic dataset and perform PCA on it:

```
>>> pca_pipe = Pipeline(
...     [
...         (
...             "std",
...             preprocessing.StandardScaler(),
...         ),
...         ("pca", PCA()),
...     ]
... )
>>> X_pca = pca_pipe.fit_transform(X)
```

Using the .named_steps attribute, we can pull properties off of the PCA portion of the pipeline:

```
>>> pca_pipe.named_steps[
...     "pca"
... ].explained_variance_ratio_
array([0.23917891, 0.21623078, 0.19265028,
       0.10460882, 0.08170342, 0.07229959,
       0.05133752, 0.04199068])
>>> pca_pipe.named_steps["pca"].components_[0]
array([-0.63368693,  0.39682566,  0.00614498,
        0.11488415,  0.58075352, -0.19046812,
       -0.21190808, -0.09631388])
```

Index

---

mutual information, 96

N
Naive Bayes classifier, 111-113
normal residuals, 228
normalizing data, 27
    (see also preprocessing data)
null values, percentage of, 21

O
optimization, model, 34
ordinal encoder, 85
ordinal values, comparing, 65
OSX, library installation on, 5
out-of-bag (OOB) error, 127
overfitting, 156

P
pair grid, 63
pairwise comparisons, 67-71
pandas
    classification calculations, 160
    column names, 51
    data standardization, 78
    DataFrame column correla-
      tion, 69-71
    determining data size, 55
    dropping rows with missing
      data, 47
    dummy variable creation, 80
    feature examination in clus-
      ters, 286
    for indicator columns, 49
    for missing data bar plot, 44
    frequency encoding, 82
    histograms with, 58
    iloc attribute, 57
    imports with, 12
    imputing missing values with,
      48
    int64 vs. Int64 types, 17
    label encoding, 81

    manual feature engineering,
      88
    ordinal category comparison,
      65
    parallel coordinates plot, 74
    profile report with, 18
    RadViz plots, 72
    scaling data to range, 79
    scatter plot generation, 59
    summary stats, 56
    updating columns, 52
parallel coordinates plot, 73
partial dependence plots, 181-185
PCA (see principal component
    analysis)
Pearson correlation, 60, 67
permutation importance, 132
PHATE (Potential of Heat-
    diffusion for Affinity-based
    Trajectory Embedding),
    268-271
pip
    in conda environment, 7
    installation of libraries with,
      5-6
pipelines, 289-293
    classification, 289-291
    imputing data with, 47
    PCA, 293
    regression, 292
Potential of Heat-diffusion for
    Affinity-based Trajectory
    Embedding (PHATE),
    268-271
precision
    discrimination threshold and,
      175
    F1 and, 165
    of classifications, 164
precision-recall curve, 167
prediction error plot, 230
preprocessing data, 27, 77-88

About the Author

Matt Harrison runs MetaSnake, a Python and Data Science training and consulting company. He has been using Python since 2000 across a breadth of domains: data science, BI, storage, testing and automation, open source stack management, finance, and search.

Colophon

The animal on the cover of *Machine Learning Pocket Reference* is the northern crested newt (*Triturus cristatus*), an amphibian found near standing water in Britain eastward through mainland Europe to Western Russia.

This newt has a gray-brown back with dark spots and a yellow-orange underside with white speckles. Males develop large jagged crests during the mating season, while females always have an orange stripe on their tails.

While not hibernating in mud or under rocks during the winter months, the northern crested newt hunts for other newts, tadpoles, young froglets, worms, insect larvae, and water snails in water and for insects, worms, and other invertebrates on land. They live for as long as 27 years and can be up to 7 inches long.

While the northern crested newt's current conservation status is designated as of Least Concern, many of the animals on O'Reilly covers are endangered; all of them are important to the world.

The cover illustration is by Karen Montgomery, based on a black and white engraving from *Meyers Kleines Lexicon*. The cover fonts are Gilroy Semibold and Guardian Sans. The text font is Adobe Minion Pro; the heading font is Adobe Myriad Condensed; and the code font is Dalton Maag's Ubuntu Mono.